ALBERT SCHWEITZER
THE DIFFICULTY OF DOING GOOD

Albert Schweitzer:
The Difficulty of Doing Good

Published by The Authors' Collective, 2017
Copyright © Patricia Morris, 2017

ISBN: 978-1-911047-66-7
e-ISBN: 978-1-911047-67-4

Also by Patricia Morris

Freud, Politics and Civilisation

Love & Sex: fifty therapy lessons

T. A. C.
LONDON

ALBERT SCHWEITZER
THE DIFFICULTY OF DOING GOOD

Patricia Morris

---

including the Lambaréné diary
of the orthopaedic surgeon

Cecil Morris

In memory of my father, Cecil Morris (1916-1991)

Acknowledgements

I OWE much to my dearest friend since childhood, Angela Brotman in Toronto, for our long discussions, her encouragement, and her invaluable clarity of thought. Hélène Schweitzer's biographer, Verena Mühlstein in Munich, was generous with her instructive and delightful conversation. Radiologist George Cohen, now in Sydney, was bounteous in sharing with me his impressions of Schweitzer when he worked with him in 1959. My thanks also for the help given to me by Romain Collot of the Maison Albert Schweitzer archives in Günsbach, and Nicole Westerdahl at the Special Collections Research Center, Syracuse University Libraries. My heartfelt gratitude to my cousin David Hirschowitz, an orthopaedic surgeon, who was able to decipher many of the medical terms hidden in my father's handwriting. Last, but not least, my thanks to those stoical friends who let me test my ideas on them and who asked all the right, often difficult, questions. Any mistakes in the text are entirely my own.

To content oneself with becoming small:
that is the only salvation and liberation.
To work in the world, asking nothing of it, or of man,
not even recognition, that is true happiness.

Albert Schweitzer
(From a sermon given at St Nicholas Church,
Strasbourg, June 1905.)

CONTENTS

Preface

THIS book was prompted by the notes my father made sixty years ago when he volunteered in 1957 at Albert Schweitzer's hospital and leper village in Lambaréné, in Gabon, central Africa.

Schweitzer, a polymath – theologian, musician, philosopher, medical doctor – began his adult life as a Lutheran pastor in a village in Alsace. He became one of the most recognised men in the world. His very name was emblematic of the heights of moral integrity to which a human being can aspire. His non-violent, environmentalist philosophy was encapsulated in his famous phrase that called for "reverence for life".

Despite all that, these days, it's a rare person who can explain why they have even heard his name. Usually, they haven't.

The first part of this book gives background material to the second part which is a transcription of the brief diary that my father kept in Lambaréné. The book ends with three poignantly self-explanatory letters that he later received from Schweitzer and from two of his co-workers. I found the letters wedged under the last page of his jottings.

Chapter 1 gives some context to Schweitzer's inspiration to go to Africa as a so-called medical missionary in 1913, and outlines the practical difficulties he overcame to establish his hospital in an equatorial jungle. Chapter 2 describes his romantic and then fraught relationship with his wife. (Coincidentally, my father was at the dockside when they bade her a sombre farewell in Lambaréné, and he was still working at the hospital when Schweitzer heard that she had died of her illness in Zurich.)

Chapter 3 deals with the problems Schweitzer had to overcome in developing his medical project. Chapter 4 outlines his relationships with some of the many remarkable women who gave him practical and emotional support. He attracted people who wanted to help him but, equally, he had unusual psychological resources. His was a rare combination of intellectual brilliance, artistic creativity, practical talent, an independence of will, a pervasive solitariness, all of which he exercised while being always surrounded by many people at close – and noisy – quarters.

Chapters 5 focuses on the vulnerability to attack of a person who risks doing the extraordinary. These difficulties were sometimes circumstantial because of the terrain, climate and the clash of cultures, and sometimes arose from European and American prejudice against his philosophy, his actions and his national origins.

Chapter 6 reveals something of the soap opera that runs in parallel to tragedy and also alludes to the complex moral choices arising out of taking from the rich to give to the poor. From its inception, Schweitzer's project in Africa was characterised by a curious moral *mésalliance*, vivid to us with hindsight. He had to affiliate himself with generous financial donors whose values his philosophy sought to undo. This was a perverse contradiction that remained inarticulate partly because it was ever-present, an inescapable white noise, and partly because he believed that one must focus on the good impulses in people, not judge and reject them for the bad.

Chapters 7, 8 and 9 outline Schweitzer's atypical venture into protest and political opinion, suggesting that here lie the real reasons for his iconic image being shifted away from the public eye. In his last years, he became vociferous in the anti-nuclear lobby, the pre-cursor to CND, that some identified with undermining the West's supremacy in the Cold War. This put him in a line of fire that in certain quarters led to verbal attacks that muddied his legacy. But that was not all.

From the period of World War I to the end of World War II, he had been closely observed because of his presumed sympathy with Germany, to which Alsace had belonged before World War I. After World War II, he was under suspicion as a Communist sympathiser who might be supporting a Soviet plot to gain access to the unique uranium being mined by Western allies in the Democratic Republic of Congo (the former Belgian Congo). Suspicion of Schweitzer mounted in the CIA, the UN and in Europe's intelligence services focussed on that region.

This goes some way towards explaining the off-key political interpretations that those in power projected on to his ethical values. Accolades and awards from philanthropic organisations continued to be showered upon him but the age of innocent idolisation was over.

The last chapters of the book attempt to unravel and then summarise narratives that are still contested, whose records are still being, or not being, de-classified in government archives. Even in its abbreviated form, the account exposes the nightmare that was happening a stone's throw from Schweitzer's experiment in benignity.

For him, the horror would only cease if we were all to change our interactions with living things. He spelt it out in his philosophy of moral activism. At the end, he could not but know that the groundswell of his ideas amongst ordinary people had been insufficient to alter the course of those who hold power. At the end, he did not go gentle into that good night.

༜

This book offers the barest discussion of Schweitzer's writings about theology and philosophy, both of them avenues into his intellectual and emotional purport. Nor is there discourse about what today we would call his practice of variations on the political theme of anarcho-pacifism, nor about his environmentalism *avant la lettre*. There is no academic analysis of Schweitzer's writings about music. He was famous throughout Europe as a musicologist, an organ-builder, a concert performer, and an expert on J.S. Bach. He said that from early childhood, music had sustained him in every way, from the spiritual – to the financial. On his regular trips to Europe from Africa, he had a gruelling touring schedule to raise money for his hospital, giving lectures about his philosophy and about Lambaréné but also giving organ recitals.

My research is limited, drawing almost entirely upon published documents and personal conversations in the languages of or about the white foreigners who kept the hospital functioning over half a century.[1]

I wanted to make my research process as transparent as possible. I've made free with footnotes, a sort of underground stream with friable banks, bubbling up here and there beneath the main story. They expose the

---

[1] Only recently has methodical research begun on uncovering and documenting the hospital's fifty years of support from international volunteers who gave their skills, labour and time. Philanthropic individuals, organisations, drug companies, church-groups and universities gave money, equipment and resources. The hospital was entirely dependent on Schweitzer's capacity to generate donations.

different directions that research actually takes in the futile attempt to compress a person's life into a linear narrative.

Throughout, the reader will be bothered, as am I, by the absent voices of the thousands of black patients who were treated at the hospital. With the exception of the writings of his biographer James Brabazon and, separately, Augustin Emane, published documentation about or by patients is scarce.[2] Over eight years, Emane interviewed about sixty Gabonese "witnesses", the doctor's patients, his employees, or those who had known them. Their interpretations ranged from Schweitzer as a white racist inducing anxiety about black inferiority, to Schweitzer as but another *nganga,* a sorcerer-healer who augmented his powers using music, rules, rituals, and assistants in white clothing.

There is almost no published record of the few local medical assistants, builders, gardeners and interpreters who were close to Schweitzer, in some cases for many years. The information is waiting to be unearthed in the extensive Schweitzer archives, barring questions of confidentiality.

---

[2] Augustin Emane, *Albert Schweitzer, une icône africaine* (Paris: Fayard, 2013), for which Emane won the *Grand prix littéraire d'Afrique noire* that year. He is an academic lawyer at the University of Nantes and was born at Schweitzer's hospital. Also, James Brabazon, *Albert Schweitzer: a comprehensive biography* (1976; Syracuse, 2000). He is not to be confused with the much younger journalist of the same name.

Introduction

IN 1913, when Schweitzer first set foot on African soil to fulfil a mission of his own devising, he had no idea what lay ahead for him and his wife, Hélène Bresslau, who accompanied him.

A relatively impecunious pastor, he had spent years working and saving to pay for his medical training in Strasbourg, all the while finding donors to finance his plan to set up a clinic in equatorial Africa. It was his wife who had first alerted him to a lecture she had attended in London about King Ludwig II's maltreatment of Africans in "the Congo". The speaker was referring to the Belgian Congo but it was common then, as now, for Europeans not to distinguish it from the French Congo and the rest of French Equatorial Africa. (The French colonial possessions in central Africa, known as *Afrique équatoriale française*, the AEF, comprised a federation including what today we know as Chad, the Central African Republic, Cameroon, the Republic of Congo, and Gabon.)

Ironically, at the end of his life, for reasons just as grave, Schweitzer was once more to concern himself deeply with the Congo, that is, the Democratic Republic of Congo whose borders, by this time, he understood well. Back at the turn of the century he was preoccupied with the debt that Europe owed "the Congo" to compensate for its colonial depredations, although whatever the compensation, it would never suffice. His own contribution would be to devote the rest of his life to alleviating physical suffering.

His medical training in Strasbourg had barely prepared him for what he was to encounter: leprosy, venereal diseases, malaria, problematic childbirths, fractures, hernias, dysentery, elephantiasis, sleeping sickness, yellow fever, tropical sores, ubiquitous intestinal worms, injuries arising from accidents or violence, infections unknown in Europe, and more.

Even so brilliant a man as Schweitzer did not spring fully-formed from the head of Zeus. Like anyone else, he learned as he went along and his ideas changed over the many years. His vocabulary and views about local "tribes" in 1920 had matured by the time that, for instance, he was supporting the nomination of Albert Luthuli for the Nobel Prize. Forty years after Schweitzer set up his first clinic on the Ogowe River, when it had become a sprawling compound with a thousand inhabitants, Clara Urquhart wrote of a hypothetical critic of the doctor:

> If he has no humility towards the genius and creativity of the man who conceived and built it all he will be critical of what he sees, and go off, thinking he has understood it all. But he might react differently if he remembered that it took Doctor Schweitzer several decades to be able to understand even something of the ways and needs of the Africans of those parts, and that much still remains a mystery to him to this day.[3]

❧

Amongst the people who say they recognise Albert Schweitzer's name from the 1950s and '60s, there are always a few who say that he may have fallen from grace

---

[3] Clara Urquhart (1906-1985), *With Dr Schweitzer in Lambaréné* (London: Harrap, 1957), p.21.

but they're not sure why. Even at the time, the reasons for the shift in attitude towards him were inchoate. From having been a household name, he just faded from view. While there isn't an explanation that would thrill a conspiracy theorist, there was often an ulterior motive behind the change in tone in the non-liberal press reports about the so-called man of God and his medical mission in Africa.

The impetus to render him invisible came from several directions at once during those last years. A jumpy CIA tried to downgrade the saintly status of the French-speaking German from Alsace because they thought he might be in bed with the Reds. Parts of the liberal lobby took the view that he was withholding a share of Western privilege and affluence by not training local people in Western medicine. Happily, none of the negative press at the time undoes his achievement, his extraordinary life and his positive effect upon many thousands of people.

His critics could not understand his concerted effort *not* to impose Western values and European clutter on Africans. They could not understand his position, in current lingo, of anti-globalisation, of pro-localisation.

At that time, it was not yet a wide-spread ethical imperative for intruders in a pristine land to avoid leaving an ecological or political footprint on non-Western cultures. Not for nothing did Rachel Carson inscribe to Schweitzer her ground-breaking work, *Silent Spring* (1962). She quoted him thus in her dedication: "Man has lost the capacity to foresee and to forestall. He will end by destroying the earth."

On the political side, there was an assumption that those unfortunate enough not to have Western style clothing, capitalism, and washing machines, *surely* wanted them because they signalled everything to which one *surely* aspired. In addition, the word was out that Schweitzer was not so much a saint as always the boss and also bossy. He didn't equate doing good with being nicey-nice. The African Nationalist movement simply labelled him a white racist.

His story exposes how morality and fame find each other against all the odds, then spawn distant progeny with dubious values. His detractors didn't read his philosophy books, had no idea why he was doing what he was doing, and weren't interested anyway. They almost deracinated his good reputation and turned off the limelight around the same time that he died on 4 September 1965. He was ninety.

His daughter Rhena thought that "the mounting criticism of his hospital during his last year seemed designed to discredit him as a critic of nuclear arms testing".[4] My own impression is that the move to discredit him for those reasons had been going on for years.

And then there is the march of history. The last words in this book, an innocent letter to my father from Schweitzer's personal assistant, nurse Ali Silver, inadvertently captures the tragedy and the irony that follows in the wake of power. It all points to the difficulty of doing good.

౼౼

There are practical obstacles and disheartening human responses that deter the average person from persisting in trying to do the right thing. Schweitzer was not an average person. He was exceptional in his capacity to retain his integrity against the odds. He was a flawed man of flesh

---

[4] Rhena Miller, "Albert Schweitzer and His Nuclear Concerns Seen Today" in *Courier,* XXI, 2 (Fall 1986), pp. 17-26.

and blood to whom one returns to experience the proximity of that rarity, a deeply ethical human being. Admirable medical and benevolent work in his name continues, thanks to the reach of the AISL in Günsbach, Alsace.[5] It has affiliates such as the ASF (the Albert Schweitzer Fellowship) based in Boston.[6] The ASF has charge of the prestigious annual Albert Schweitzer Prize for Humanitarianism, awarded to individuals who have made outstanding contributions to humanity and the environment.

While Schweitzer is no longer a household name, he is still the subject of a large amount of research at any one time.[7] No single piece of work can be wide-ranging enough to encompass the breadth of his achievements and his argument, the moral impetus of his practical mission, and above all why in its pure form it could not survive the death of the man himself. It turns out to be difficult to do good.

---

[5] AISL: *Association Internationale pour l'œuvre du docteur Albert Schweitzer de Lambaréné* – the International Association of the Albert Schweitzer Hospital. Organisations around the world that use Schweitzer's name include the Albert Schweitzer Children's Villages in Germany, and Larry and Gwen Mellon's Albert Schweitzer Hospital in Haiti.

[6] The ASF, founded in 1940 with a remit to perpetuate humanitarian service, is today a large philanthropic, medical organisation with a national office in Boston, Mass., USA.

[7] There is a plethora of information hidden in barely examined archives. After her father's death, Schweitzer's daughter sold his papers to Syracuse University which thus holds the largest Schweitzer archive in north America. He habitually made notes in a pocket notebook of which the University Library has 123. There are copies at the Günsbach archives in France that, aside from thousands of patient records, also hold some 70,000 letters written to Schweitzer, 10,000 letters from him, and 40,000 relevant photographs. There are also Schweitzer archives in Switzerland and Germany.

After World War II, by which time his name was familiar to everyone, nobody was surprised (although he himself was) that he was awarded the Nobel Peace Prize. It is touching to discover that the Gabonese have never forgotten him. Every child at school there is taught about him and his philosophy calling for "reverence for life". In 2013 Gabon celebrated the centenary of Schweitzer's arrival in Lambaréné, honouring him for being a man who lived his life in the service of others.

Unfortunately, the Gabonese celebrations may have partaken more of wish than of fulfilment. Large donations in the mid-1970s had allowed for the complete rebuilding of Schweitzer's original, hand-made, low-tech jungle hospital. After independence in 1960, although later funded partly by the Gabonese government, the hospital's functioning depended on foreign charity – as it always had done. Consequently, a hundred years on, while most of the staff were African, the directors, representing the source of the funding, continued to be white and foreign. Accusations of racism came to a head after the millennium, along with counter-accusations that staff were stealing hospital funds and that members of the government were implicated. In 2011, the first Gabonese director was appointed, Antoine Nziengui. Despite his best efforts there remained the problem of unpaid staff and the disappearance of hospital resources. At the end of 2016 there were reports that the hospital had more or less ceased functioning.

PART I

1

The Mission

WE all like to think that we are good people, that we are amongst the few who uphold kind, honest and moral views in this wicked world. We want justice for all. We want wholesome food on our children's plates, the least polluting petrol to put in our tanks, the most worker-friendly company to make our jeans. So much for the expression of our values. But how many of us try, consciously, every day, to lead a completely moral life?

When he was about twenty, Schweitzer decided that he would do what he liked for the next ten years and then, when he was thirty, he would begin to live a life consistent with the teachings of Jesus. On the basis of his extensive reading in not just German and French but also Latin, Greek and Hebrew, he demonstrated logically that Jesus was not Christ. He argued on the basis of his research findings that Jesus's ethics were not his own illuminating invention but were consistent with the Judaic code of the time. What's more, Jesus had regarded himself not as the Christ but as a herald of the imminent Kingdom of God on earth, perhaps a prophet. When Jesus realised that he had been wrong about that imminence, he submitted to capture and crucifixion.[8]

---

[8] Albert Schweitzer, *The Quest of the Historical Jesus: a critical study of its progress from Reimarus to Wrede* (Augsburg Fortress, 1906); Albert Schweitzer, *The Psychiatric Study of Jesus* (1913), his published doctoral thesis. Also, *Paul and his Interpreters, a critical history,* trans. W. Montgomery (Adam & Charles Black, 1912).

Schweitzer's book of 1906 was a bolt from the blue for the church establishment. This was to make it a little complicated for him to find a mission that would accept his application to serve. Meanwhile, he earned a living as a Lutheran pastor in Alsace, became a much-travelled organist in different parts of Europe, and a respected, published, interpreter of Bach.

When he was thirty the time had come for him to honour his pledge to himself to follow the teachings of Jesus. The board of a Protestant missionary association, the *Société des missions évangéliques de Paris* (the Paris Missionary Society) at last gingerly accepted his application albeit that one of its members resigned in protest. Schweitzer would be allowed to set up a medical clinic at a station at Andende in French Equatorial Africa. There were conditions. These included that he pay his own expenses and that he refrain from preaching. The committee was concerned that his odd theological ideas would corrupt the Mission's African converts. (A survey much later concluded that the mission actually made no genuine converts.) Schweitzer settled for this compromise.

He used the delay that had been imposed on him to study further to gain a specialist qualification in tropical medicine. He continued to look for sponsors and saved whatever he could earn. He later said that his first books on Bach paid for his first hospital buildings in Africa.[9] He estimated the amount he would need to see him through two years in the jungle before he would have to come

---

[9] Norman Cousins, *Dr Schweitzer of Lambaréné* (Harper, 1960), p.126. Albert Schweitzer, *J. S. Bach, Le Musicien-Poète*, introd., C. M. Widor (Leipzig: Breitkopf & Härtel with P. Costellot, 1905).

back to replenish the coffers. The mortality rate for white people in the region in 1913 was twenty per cent annually. If he knew the statistic, he ignored it. He had not the faintest idea what was in store for him when he set sail on this wild expedition.

He was accompanied, as was her wish, by his new wife, Hélène Bresslau. She was an emancipated, educated woman who had taken the precaution of doing a year's nursing training.

When they reached the mission station in French Equatorial Africa, nothing had been prepared for them, not even accommodation cleared of infestations of insects of tropical proportions. They were left to their own devices. Medical expertise was a fraction of what they needed to survive, let alone to establish a medical centre. They scrubbed down and white-washed a chicken shed. This was Schweitzer's first clinic. Half a century later it had evolved into a unique compound in another location upstream, directly on the banks of the Ogowe River, this time easily accessed by water – the only way to travel through dense, ancient jungle.

Schweitzer proved himself to be a creative architect and builder. His problem-solving innovations were subsequently copied elsewhere in the region. He aligned his buildings parallel to the passage of the sun across the equator, east-west, so that the roofing gave perpetual shade. He designed double-layered floors to allow for air circulation, and pitched rooves for hot air to rise through porous, canvas ceilings. There were no windows.[10] The

---

[10] Much later, Goldwyn writes that the renovations to the operating theatre – paid for by Prince Rainier of Monaco – included the insertion in a screen wall of a small swinging segment to let out insects, to respect Schweitzer's call for "reverence for life". However, "the nurses do use an insecticide

long sides of the wards and residential buildings were mainly mesh screens creating cross ventilation, light, and protection from insects. Curtains could be drawn for privacy. The buildings were arranged on terraces so that the rain water from the frequent tropical storms flowed down to the river, minimizing the formation of pools in which mosquitoes would breed.

By the time of Schweitzer's death in 1965, the compound had some seventy hand-made buildings with a separate leper village (that he had named *Le Village Lumière*) about half a mile west of the hospital. The main hospital comprised separate sections for out-patients, an operating theatre, and the staff's living quarters. Schweitzer's own spartan room was the same as everyone else's.

People called it a hospital as a kind of shorthand which was unfortunate since it was criticised later for its inadequacy as a hospital. My father, Cecil Morris, put it succinctly. He said it wasn't a hospital but a place for people to stay when they needed medical attention and had travelled far from their home village to get it. There were those who

> really do not understand what Schweitzer has built up and what he has worked for. Those [critical] people, with good intentions, probably want to change the place into a more modern hospital. It is not realized that the nomenclature 'Hospital' is incorrect and the real intention is an out-patient service with facilities for the odd

---

but they are careful to employ it after checking that Dr. Schweitzer is not around to witness it." Robert M. Goldwyn, M.D. (1931-2010), *The Goldwyn Diary of November and December 1960, at the Albert Schweitzer Hospital, Lambaréné, Gabon.* (Entries for 9 and 15 November 1960.) Goldwyn was twenty-nine when he volunteered at the hospital for two months. He was amused to learn that because he was adept at his work, the staff assumed he was in his forties.

emergencies. Although there are so-called [hospital] beds, this is really a board and lodging facility.[11]

This "out-patient service" amounted to accommodation and medical treatment for the patient, accommodation for his or her *gardiens*, and for all of them daily rations of a staple food, maize or rice, and by the late 1950s, manioc or bananas. Patients and their *gardiens* were expected to pay the hospital the equivalent of a pound sterling, if they could, or else in kind, with their labour. *Gardiens* looked after the patient whom they accompanied, assisted around the hospital and vegetable gardens, and helped keep the forest from encroaching on the orchards.[12] Anyone at the hospital was permitted to help themselves to whatever they had the energy to pick.

The production of a source of food was difficult. One of Schweitzer's first lessons in 1913 was that the hospital could exist only as long as he could provide a staple food for the staff and patients. The vegetable gardens and fruit trees were maintained to the end, with Schweitzer's persistent personal oversight of them. It was widely known that the plantation was a wonder.

In illustration of Schweitzer's micro-management, radiologist Dr George Cohen told me of a medical meeting in 1959 that Schweitzer allowed to be interrupted

---

[11] See the diary transcript in Part II, below.

[12] The encroachment of the jungle was a cause for toil. When the plastic surgeon Dr Jack Penn (1909-1996) made his first visit to Lambaréné in early 1956, he recorded that the invading growth had begun to choke the orchard and Schweitzer was having to move some of his trees. This corrective work must have been necessary just at that time because Schweitzer had been in Europe in 1955. His close assistant, an ailing Emma Haussknecht, holding the fort, had been supervising the two-year long building of the new leper village. She died on 1 June 1956.

freely by a gardener wanting to discuss the removal of a branch from a tree in the orchard. Schweitzer went down to inspect the branch while the meeting waited for his return.[13]

This could hardly be said to resemble any other hospital one has ever heard of. When the modern hospital replaced the old one after Schweitzer's death, instead of growing, it began to fail.[14]

---

[13] Author's conversation with Dr George Cohen (b.1927) in Sydney, Australia, to which he had emigrated in 1977 from Johannesburg. Cohen was 31 when he volunteered at Lambaréné in 1959. In the early 1970s he organised a "flying doctors" project, Harry's Angels, between Johannesburg and Swaziland.

[14] With money raised by the Albert Schweitzer Fellowship, Rhena Schweitzer Miller and Dr David Miller led the transformation of the hospital after Schweitzer's death in 1965. Several staff members were unhappy about this. Dr Isao Takahashi, who ran the leper village, returned to Japan in 1966. Nurse Ali Silver, having served at the hospital for twenty years, became the archivist at the Günsbach house in Alsace. Dr Walter Munz, whom Schweitzer had appointed as medical director, returned to Europe in 1969 but maintained his association with the hospital.

2

Marriage to Hélène Bresslau

MY father happened to be in Lambaréné when Hélène Bresslau Schweitzer was visiting for the last time. She was then seventy-eight and had been ill for many years. Always a keen traveller, for most of her life her base had been in Germany or Switzerland. In 1957 she had probably come to Lambaréné knowing it would be her last visit and that her end was near. On the day of her departure from Lambaréné, my father joined a large and silent crowd gathered along the river at the hospital's dock to bid her farewell. Accompanied by a nurse, she was to take a plane back to Europe to receive specialised medical attention. Within days news came that she had died in Zurich.

Schweitzer heard about her death the day afterwards. It happened to be the eve of my father's departure from Lambaréné and he records with interest Schweitzer's typically unsentimental response to the news. There was no announcement, no emotional display, no discussion. To some it may have seemed that Schweitzer had no feelings.

My own interpretation is that for all his reticence, he must have been overwhelmed by the momentousness of her passing. Her death put an end to a long life-time's reminder of his failure to live up to his own – and certainly her – ideals. For some seventy years, their relationship had been in turn his happy secret, his secret care, his Chinese water-torture, his cross.

In his youth, he had always said that he would never marry. By this one may suppose that he did not want the constraints and obligations that came with marriage and that he did not want children. It may not be coincidental that soon after their only, unplanned, child was born, he in effect left the marriage and had hardly any connection with his daughter until she initiated a rapprochement after her mother died.

Hélène Bresslau and Albert Schweitzer had been formally introduced in 1898 when she was nineteen and he was twenty-three. On 22 March 1902, they made a secret undertaking of commitment to each other but quite what this meant, nobody knows. After their thirteen-year courtship, which was never acknowledged as such, perhaps least of all by himself, he reneged on his pledges to himself. They married the year before they left for Africa. Five years later, when she was nearly forty, she was pregnant.

In certain respects, Hélène Bresslau and Schweitzer were very unlike. Her patriotic German parents were secular Jews. Her father, a highly-regarded university professor of history, had his children baptised as Lutherans so that the family would not be stigmatised in anti-Semitic Europe. It made no difference later when the Nazis came to power. Hélène and her daughter, then in occupied France, had to flee the country.

Schweitzer came from a line of Lutheran pastors, austere, low-church and liberal. "Schweitzer" means "Swiss" in German. His ancestral family came from Switzerland but his immediate family was from Alsace, a culturally complex region with its own dialects. It became part of Germany in 1870, five years before Schweitzer was born, and was returned to France after Germany's defeat in World War I.

Schweitzer's family spoke Alsatian German but had a strong affinity with France. The French regarded the Alsatians as Germans and the Germans as inferior to the French. Many Alsatians lived in France. Schweitzer was close to his first cousin, Anne-Marie (1882-1969), the daughter of Schweitzer's father's older brother, a renegade intellectual and *roué* who moved to France in his youth to avoid his father's insistence that he enter the church. Anne-Marie Schweitzer's son was the philosopher, Jean-Paul Sartre (1905-1980). In Sartre's *Les Mots* (1963), he describes how even as a child on a family visit to the Schweitzers in Alsace, he was allowed to enjoy a sense of social superiority to his hosts.

Hélène Bresslau was a well-travelled, well-educated, emancipated, single woman who in her twenties taught languages and worked for several years as what today we would call a government social worker. Between 1905 and 1909 she was employed as an "orphan inspector" in Strasbourg and in 1907 helped start a home for "unwed" mothers. She was always interested in Schweitzer's activities even when they were physically separated, as they frequently were, not just by propriety but by their work commitments. He used her as his confidante, describing his frustrations, disappointments or exhaustion from over-work. She was his sounding board and his source of encouragement. She discussed with him and helped proof and translate some of his writings. While he spoke Alsatian German and French, and could read classical languages, he was a relatively poor linguist, whereas languages were her *forté*.

He was tall, handsome, strong, well-built, brilliant, talented, thoughtful, a born leader, a principled, liberal

Christian. Numbers of educated, exciting women orbited him, several were close friends, and with one of them, during the many years of his pre-marital association with Hélène Bresslau, he even holidayed regularly. Hélène betrayed no possessiveness of him and appeared to accept his decision to remain a bachelor.

His preaching and musicianship were as much appreciated in small provincial congregations as they were in the sophisticated circles of Strasbourg, Paris, Barcelona and beyond. Cosima Wagner, for example, whom he met when she came to stay with her daughter Eva in Strasbourg, took a liking to the young musician and is said to have given him a few quiet tips about how to speak and behave in high society.

Meanwhile, when he wrote slightly shame-faced letters to Hélène Bresslau, mentioning having spent time with one or another – often married – woman, she always responded that he was at liberty to do so. He felt the need to confess to her but it isn't always clear why, or to what he was confessing.

Perhaps it was when their sexual relationship had advanced somewhat that he seemed to find the secret of their intimacy playfully arousing in itself. He might instruct Hélène in advance, for instance, what she should wear or not wear when they met at a public gathering. He might joke, but not without some earnest intent, that he was looking about to find a good man for her to marry and then point one out – presumably the most hilariously unlikely candidate. While he showed his gratitude for her love of him, one senses his uneasiness about his not reciprocating in kind. He never told her he loved her in the way she loved him. He was never seduced away from his life-long assertion that he would never marry. Until he married her.

Her magnetism in the relationship perhaps came from her capacity to be faithful, devoted, reassuring, and simultaneously, always slightly turned away from him. He may have had to travel often for his work but equally, he could never assume she was at his beck and call. She often put a distance between them, working far away, taking travel breaks with companions, and, late in their courtship, staying in spa towns and mountain resorts while he laboured. She was often slightly incapacitated, perhaps with backache, or fatigue, or symptoms of tuberculosis, or illnesses that had no name. She knew how to be physically fragile, the injured little bird brought to life by the big bear that he could be for her even when he was worn out and despairing. In their early years as a secret couple, he was drawn to her fragility presumably by the same pastoral impulse that once impelled him to devise a project to look after Alsatian orphans. (Only bureaucratic red tape had stopped him. Then his plan to go to Africa consolidated.)

In the early days, she seems never to have lost her balance between neediness and independence, never to have exasperated him beyond endurance, as was to occur later. She was a forceful personality but Schweitzer was always dominant. At first, she found this seductive, as did most people. Once they were married, she became jealous that everyone found him seductive. She felt rejected. After about eight difficult years, it was all but over except for the show of it. She resisted divorce, and that rather suited him.

For almost ten years while they courted, from 1902 to the end of 1911, they kept their relationship a close secret. On 22 December 1911, he wrote to her parents for permission to marry their daughter and at the same time acknowledged that his plan was to go to Africa where they would join their lives "in common work".[15] He said that he understood the sacrifice he was asking of her parents but they had long thought it through and, he said, "We belong together". He would "strive to be hers in deep gratitude, to my last breath". He didn't say that he loved her.

Her parents assented. When the engagement was announced, his friends and family were astonished. His sister was angry and believed Hélène Bresslau had trapped him. He seemed to lose his bearings for a while, and unusually, himself became ill.

Biographers have offered a number of opinions regarding why he married her and few of them include love. The Paris Missionary Society wrote to him that if he took a nurse to help him in his work at the station at Andende, they would be pleased if he were married to her. They married in the spring of 1912 and a year later they embarked for Africa.

They lived under brutally difficult circumstances. There were countless tribulations in establishing the medical clinic in Lambaréné. No sooner had they organised themselves than, the next year, World War I broke out and they were put under house arrest as enemy aliens in a French colony.

Schweitzer used this enforced stasis to begin writing what was to become his two-volume *Philosophy of Civilisation*. The completed work clarified his argument about so-called civilisation's technological advances in contrast to its ethical retrogression. Apparent progress rested heavily on past, much greater, achievements. He

---

[15] Rhena Schweitzer Miller (ed.), *The Albert Schweitzer – Hélène Bresslau Letters 1902-1912* (Syracuse University Press, 2003).

proposed an optimistic means to build a moral world, summed up by what he termed "reverence for life".

After a few months, to appease the demands of local people and also to serve the French soldiers posted in the region, they were permitted to resume their medical services. In 1917, they were transported to France in a convoy of ships and then interned in concentration camps. At last, with Schweitzer ill with dysentery and his wife half way through a pregnancy, they got back to war-ravaged Alsace in 1918. He was allowed to become a French citizen and started work at Strasbourg's Municipal Hospital. He also resumed his curate's post at St Nicholas, which came with accommodation. On 13 October 1918, he gave his first sermon since his departure for Africa five and a half years before. Their only child, Rhena, was born on his 44th birthday on 14 January 1919.

In October 1919, he was in Barcelona playing the organ for the *Orféo Català*. The following Easter, 1920, he was lecturing in Sweden, the first of several working tours there. That summer, his wife was writing to him from Heidelberg. In 1921, he gave concerts in Sweden, Switzerland and Germany. By the end of 1923 he had received an honorary doctorate in theology from the University of Zurich, had made working tours of Britain and elsewhere, had published a best-selling book about the Lambaréné hospital as well as two substantial volumes of philosophy.[16] Above all, he had paid off his debts. The marriage was over but they kept up appearances.

---

[16] *On the Edge of the Primeval Forest [Zwischen Wasser und Urwald]* (Black, 1922); and *The Decay and Restoration of Civilization* and *Civilization and Ethics* (Black, 1923), published together as *Philosophy and Civilization* (Macmillan, 1949).

He built her a house, ready for habitation on 1 May 1923.[17] It was in a place of her choice that she knew well, Königsfeld in the Black Forest, the spa town that still boasts a "therapeutic climate". So – Lambaréné *not*. She had spent recuperative time in Königsfeld while he studied or worked to raise money before their first voyage to Africa. How did she ever pay for her sojourns in health resorts throughout her life? Nobody says. After they were married, he must have paid the bills out of the money he raised on his working visits to Europe, lecturing and giving organ recitals. Meanwhile, he felt no resentment that his own life-style was ascetic. He took it for granted that he patched his clothes and made his own notebooks out of paper scraps and string. He would have lived that way anyway, whether or not he had to support his wife and daughter.

In 1924, he returned to Lambaréné without them. In the years following, Hélène Bresslau would join him infrequently, supposedly because her delicate health could not tolerate the climate or the voyage, it isn't clear which. Over thirty-three years, she made eight visits, varying from a few weeks to a few months in duration. Her periods staying at the hospital were sometimes short: the climate was more tolerable nearer the coast where they had friends who could accommodate her. Her longest sojourn was during World War II when she made a spectacularly dramatic and danger-ridden voyage from Lisbon to Lambaréné, apparently suffering no physical ill-effects from the rigours of the journey. She had crossed France, Spain and Portugal on her own, boarded a boat at Lisbon port and arrived unannounced at the Lambaréné hospital dock in the dead of night on 2 August 1941. In

---

[17] Today the house is the museum, *Das Albert Schweitzer Haus.*

mid-1946 she left to join her daughter in Königsfeld. It was the most extensive period that the couple had lived together since their internments during World War I.

The legend of her ill-health has holes in it. Her life-style often contradicted it, although that could be explained by the fluctuation of symptoms of tuberculosis. She supposedly couldn't return to Africa with her husband in 1924 because of ill-health but her biographer Marxsen points out that in October that year she helped at the Hospital Aid Association in Basel and in August 1926 she was at the Medical Missionary Institute in Tubingen doing a three-week course in tropical medicine.[18]

The persona of the delicate woman served several purposes. It evoked sympathy and, for someone bent on keeping up appearances, it perfectly explained why she could not live with her husband. Since her youth, Hélène Bresslau had had an appetite for travel for which she never lost her reserves of energy, or for that matter, the mysterious financial means with which to replenish it. She had seen much of Europe by the late 1930s. She was now about fifty, and their daughter, Rhena, had finished school. They moved house – to Riverside Drive in New York, America. Rhena had grown into a well-educated, eligible young woman, determined not to repeat the pattern of being an old parent. She was soon engaged, married, and having children.

Hélène Bresslau busied herself with a new enterprise which by happy coincidence also justified the enforced marital separation. She toured several American cities giving public lectures about Lambaréné, illustrating her

---

[18] Patti Marxsen, *Hélène Schweitzer: A Life of Her Own* (Syracuse University Press, 2015), p.78. Also, Verena Mühlstein, *Hélène Schweitzer Bresslau: Ein Leben für Lambaréné* (Beck, 2001).

talks with a slide show. Unlike her husband, she spoke English well. She told the story of how in 1913 they had established the *urwaldspitals,* the jungle-hospital, which still continued to provide its unique service. Her account impressed prospective American donors.[19] By 1939 there was sufficient impetus to set up the Albert Schweitzer Fellowship (ASF) to raise money for the hospital and to disseminate the principles of "reverence for life."

At the same time in 1939, Schweitzer, in his remote eyrie, was aware of the political crisis festering in Europe. He advised his wife and daughter to stay in America. They ignored his advice. Hélène Bresslau returned to France, moving in with her daughter and her new son-in-law. None of them could have predicted how timely had been her campaign to arouse the interest and generosity of American sponsors. World War II broke out and the hospital found itself dependent on American aid.

It is an unexamined curiosity that says much for Schweitzer's leadership, that during the war he maintained his hospital compound as a non-political safe haven. He harboured the wives and children of both Free French and Vichy colonial soldiers who were enemies just beyond its confines.

In those last days with his wife in 1957, Schweitzer must have known that he would never see her again. Perhaps it seemed to him that whatever hardships he had had to endure in Africa, and they were legion, nothing

---

[19] In 1946, the prominent American missionary Emory Ross (1887-1973) and his wife Myrta were probably the first of the post-war fund-raisers to fly to Lambaréné to see the place for themselves. Ten years later, generous donors who did likewise were the American Lawrence Gussman (1916-2004) and his wife Kaye.

compared to what she had represented in his long life. Her handling of their failed marriage had tested to the limit his struggle to follow the teachings of Jesus. She became his nemesis, an angry woman who attached herself to him with bonds that cut. Even though they actually rarely saw each other, here and there, tales crop up about her temper tantrums when they did meet, or when they did not, little scenes she created because of her resentment about her exclusion from his life. Her pride could not tolerate any dilution of the social status that she believed was owed to the wife of an important man.

Although Schweitzer travelled abroad nearly every year, speaking to hundreds, thousands, of people, he had the demeanour of a man uncomfortable in a throng. He disliked appearing unaccompanied at a public gathering, disliked even entering a crowded room on his own. His companions and assistants, often women, were a buffer between himself and the ordinary stuff of life. Whether or not he was managing a kind of introversion, the effect was to add to his gravitas. People paid attention to him.

He had always had a female entourage. His wife's jealousy regarding other women was an emotion she had kept in check before they were married but not afterwards. Of jealousies amongst and between those other women, who often knew each other well, we hear nothing.

The couple's relationship after World War I bore no resemblance to what it had been in those *fin de siècle* years. Then she had been a free woman, a "New Woman", inviting the good-looking pastor to join her bicycle club when those new-fangled machines had been affordable for just a few years. She had supported his eccentric idea about never marrying just as she had supported his outlandish missionary plans. Everything had changed between them since then except that they still had a secret from the wider world. Now their secret was not that they were intimate but that they were divorced in all but name.

Perhaps he was difficult to live with. He was known even in his youth in Alsace for the occasional verbal lashings that would spring from his impatience or moral outrage. For all his famous charm and thoughtful kindness, his irascibility is often mentioned in the literature because it contradicts expectations of a saint's state of permanent spiritual beatitude, and if he wasn't a saint, a short temper is not what admirers want of their idol. Nor was he proud of it. On the other hand, he had never been one to bear a grudge and as he grew older, he made a point of apologising after his outbursts. He was remorseful not only for his moral failure to exercise restraint but for having been plain ill-mannered. Perhaps the real surprise is that his default mood was an even temper, given that he was so brilliant, a polymath, a perfectionist, a workaholic, and that compared to him, most people around him must have seemed to him to be dull, bumbling sluggards.

Hélène Bresslau's reproach cast him in a bad light and he had no defence. After just a few years of marriage, he had rejected her at her most vulnerable hour. She had been abandoned by a selfish man who pursued his own interests and left her to fend for herself with a child in whom he showed no interest. He revelled in the adulation he received from attractive women and admiring men, and raked in awards from powerful institutions wanting to identify themselves as philanthropic. He charmed everyone with his saintly philosophising but she was not taken in. That was how she saw it.

3

Noah's Ark: Adoninalongo

> *. . . a stranger arriving there unprepared*
> *could be forgiven for imagining*
> *that he had stumbled on Noah's Ark.*
> Clara Urquhart (1957), p.9.

LONG before he returned to Africa in 1924, Schweitzer knew that he would have to find a better site if he was going to continue with his hospital plans. He would disengage from the Paris Mission at Andende, the original 1913 inland site. He acquired permission to use two hundred and twenty-two acres (ninety hectares) of more suitable riverside land, three kilometres upriver. The name of the locality is Adoninalongo but his hospital has always been called by the name of the nearby island town, Lambaréné, which at the time was a forty-minute boat ride downstream.

The first person whom Schweitzer brought to help him was the son of a friend, a young Englishman, Noel Gillespie. He interrupted his Oxford degree to join Schweitzer. They embarked on 14 February 1924, spending time in several West African ports along the way before they arrived in Lambaréné on 19 April. The old "hospital" at the Paris Mission station was in ruins. With difficulty, Schweitzer found a few local men who were interested in employment as builders. They repaired the old buildings so that he could resume his medical services while he supervised building at the new site.

Over the following three years, Schweitzer designed, oversaw and helped labour to erect the first five buildings at Adoninalongo. Countless European assumptions had to be abandoned at the dock – literally, for they had to build one in order to begin.

Nothing was simple. The jungle was impenetrable. Many trees had the girth of motor cars: their stabilizing roots and the undergrowth could be the height of a man. Hardware, materials, equipment and labour were difficult to come by. European machinery with moving parts corroded in the damp air. Anything made of softwood was soon demolished by termites. Every item had to be transported in small boats that could navigate between the waterways, avoiding crocodiles and hippopotami. Water was disease ridden. Sun-stroke was a hazard. Things animal or vegetable could drop on your head from the green canopy overhead. There were jungle predators from mammals to insects. The climate was like a sauna. Frequent tropical storms caused havoc. Fortunately, nature provided lightening conductors in the form of kapok trees that towered two hundred feet over the jungle. Schweitzer left them in place at strategic points in the compound.

Every nail was a precious artefact – but not as durable, or as stationary, as a well-designed hardwood dove-tail joint. Local people were randomly acquisitive: tools would vanish if not carefully monitored. Food that was not locked away would disappear.

Ordinary cows and sheep, ordinary staple crops, could not survive in the terrain. One of his earliest lessons was that there would be no hospital if he could not provide staple food for patients, their families, and the staff. A staple food had to be imported.[20] He experimented with various alternatives and by the 1920s had become an astute importer of rice from the Far East.

On 21 January 1927, the new dockside hospital at Adoninalongo was ready to receive its first cases. Patients at the old buildings near the Paris Mission station were transported upstream in several pirogues, accompanied by members of staff.[21] The patients were overcome by the luxurious novelty of dry, house-like rooms with mosquito netting and cool wooden floors.

Patients were not lodged in wards determined by their diagnosis, as would have been the case in a Western hospital, but according to their ethnic group. Already Schweitzer understood the need, wherever it was apt, to respect the customs of the indigenous cultures.

During World War II, de Gaulle's Free French centre of operations was in French Equatorial Africa where they were fighting it out with Vichy soldiers.[22] British and German warships patrolled the ports. As a result, the hospital could receive none of its usual cargo deliveries of

---

[20] Schweitzer kept a permanent rice reserve of not less than 20 tons. (Urquhart (1957), p.41.)

[21] In their journals, the hospital's visitors (my father included) frequently misspell the name of the dugout canoe, the pirogue, as "piroque". Perhaps the error arises from an association with the word "barque".

[22] On 5 November 1940, Free French forces successfully subdued the Vichy garrison in Lambaréné town. On 10 November 1940, Libreville was captured from Vichy forces and on 12 November, Port Gentil surrendered. Governor Georges Masson committed suicide: against his own wishes he had earlier capitulated to Vichy, under pressure from Bishop Louis Tardy and the French residents. In De Gaulle's "Brazzaville Declaration" at the town's conference of Free French leaders in January 1944, he promised equality and the vote to the people of French colonies – but not independence.

food or medical provisions and Schweitzer had to face the possibility of the whole enterprise ending because of starvation. Fortunately, American ships came to Schweitzer's rescue, delivering supplies. Later, the British navy helped de Gaulle's Free French vanquish Vichy in the region. Schweitzer never ceased to express his gratitude to America for coming to his hospital's rescue.

৵৽

"To a visitor from a big city the word 'hospital' conjures up visions of white walls, shining steel, snow-white bedding, quiet, and order."[23] Thus wrote Clara Urquhart in her book of 1957.

There was, to be sure, just such a "modern" hospital downstream from Adoninalongo, in the middle of Lambaréné town. It wasn't Schweitzer's. This hospital had been built after 1947, and was funded, or rather, under-funded, by the colonial government of the AEF. It was staffed by local employees and was run by a young white man, the sole person with medical training, Dr Weissberg. Its wards were almost empty.

The young doctor and Schweitzer developed mutual sympathy for their respective professional vexations. Their good relationship grew despite an inauspicious beginning when Dr Weissberg asked Schweitzer whether he enjoyed hunting. Schweitzer made use of Weissberg's hospital refrigerator for drugs and medical samples, and Weissberg borrowed Schweitzer's trained international staff members. Weissberg had no white staff. He said that the problem with his black staff was that they were uninterested in healing a patient from a rival ethnic group.

---

[23] Urquhart (1957), pp. 21-22.

Their intense ethnic bonds cancelled any neutral dedication to the work itself, something that Westerners take for granted. Schweitzer circumvented this difficulty by using mainly white medical and administrative staff. He trained a few black assistants who dealt with patients selectively or who were not members of rival ethnic groups. They became indispensable to him.[24]

Rather than go to the new government hospital, local people chose rather to go to Schweitzer's village-like, hand-built hospital. It provided separate accommodations that put together families belonging to friendly ethnic groups. To the Westerner, nothing about the place suggested the word "hospital". Animals walked about the compound, even into the buildings. Half-naked women squatted on the ground just outside the patients' rooms, cooking meals.[25]

Finding food throughout the region was problematic at any time. In their home villages, people knew where to forage and might even also grow a few vegetables in small, guarded clearings in the forests. It was dangerous to eat food served by strangers and this was not only superstition. One had to be skilled at de-toxifying certain wild roots by preparing them in particular, time-

[24] Brabazon mentions two medical assistants who remained for many years, both named Joseph, and also a head gardener named Evounghe. (Brabazon, 1976), p.374 and p.426. In his diary, my father mentions a pirogue oarsmen by name, Kalomutoo, with the suggestion that he had a certain status in the hospital transport system.

[25] Goldwyn wrote: "There is no common kitchen. Each family prepares its own food for fear of poisoning . . . Many poisonings occur in the villages. . . often over women, property." (4 November 1960.) "[Providing a medical service] in the jungle is a humbling experience. One should always suspect poison and treat for it and then look for other causes." (23 November 1960.

consuming, ways. We know for instance from Henry Morton Stanley's journals of his fury on discovering that his white officers in this region caused the death of a group of local bearers by having them eat roots that they had not been allowed the necessary time to make safe to consume.[26]

Despite the appearance of disorder to the outsider, Schweitzer's hospital was run according to a strict system of regulations. Every morning the rules were read out to the patients in their several different languages. It was not always possible to anticipate where a rule might be necessary but where they had to be made, they were. There are many instances of Schweitzer having to dispel his despair, such as when a patient removed his antiseptic dressings to cool a wound in the river or to show the family where the illness was coming out; or when a female patient being treated for a venereal disease spent the night entertaining a pirogue-load of visitors; or when patients obligingly took the hospital's medication as well as the disabling concoctions brought in by a sorcerer-healer.

Often the medical challenge comprised just dealing with the advanced state to which the illness had developed by the time the person sought help. Schweitzer noticed the difference between European and African patients, the quiet stoicism with which the latter suffered before coming for medical help.

There were two different treatment centres in the compound. There was the hospital, and there were the facilities for lepers. The lepers were long-term patients, staying about three and a half years, and had separate

---

[26] See Tim Jeal's superb *Stanley: The Impossible Life of Africa's Greatest Explorer* (Yale, 2008).

living quarters. Some of them worked in the main hospital or plied the pirogues that were the means of transport to and from the hospital. With the money awarded for his 1952 Nobel Peace Prize, Schweitzer built a new leper village to house a hundred and seventy lepers and about two hundred and thirty of their accompanying *gardiens*. By that time, lepers were effectively treated with sulphones, drugs first used for leprosy in 1945. The great success of the leper village was another reason that the media paid increasing attention to Schweitzer from the 1950s onwards.

The main hospital comprised about three hundred and fifty patients and their families who accompanied them, totalling about a thousand transitory inhabitants. There were about twenty-six wards, each named after a philanthropist or valued staff member. Each ward housed thirty patients and their relatives. The frames of the wooden beds were built high to provide storage space underneath for possessions, water, wood, and sometimes chickens.[27]

The doctors performed about five hundred operations each year, sometimes as many as fifty in one month, during daylight hours. The walls of the operating theatre were mesh screens facilitating the ingress of natural light, air-flow and the scrutiny of anyone passing. There was no electricity worth mentioning.[28] The noisy hospital

---

[27] Chickens, aside from their nutritional value, conveniently, eat insects. Recent research suggests that a chemical emitted by chicken feathers is a mosquito deterrent.

[28] Both Dr Robert Goldwyn in 1960 and Dr George Cohen said that the X-ray facilities were inadequate. Nevertheless, while there, Cohen made a radiological finding. It had been thought that there was no guinea worm sickness (*Dracunculus medinensis*) in the Congo basin area but his research demonstrated that it had previously been misdiagnosed. His X-

generator was turned on only in order to take an X-ray or to illuminate the operating theatre in night-time emergencies. The din awakened the whole village.

Patients lived there with their relatives for as long as it took to be healed. One of Schweitzer's many non-medical headaches entailed determining who stayed on for the free board and lodging or which patients might discharge themselves before they were quite well. Some families just dumped someone sick or old to die there, and hurriedly departed. Sometimes a *gardien* remained to help in the hospital in order to show their appreciation of a sick relative having been made well.

The patients were usually forest-dwelling hunter-gatherers belonging to several ethnic groups, some fiercely territorial and bellicose. In the wider region, there were more than twenty-five ethnic groups, each with its own language. Along the proximate reaches of the Ogowe River there were several groups using the hospital, especially two dominant rivals, the Fang (or Pahoin) who were cannibals and the Galwa, who were not. (Obviously, the life-style of these jungle-dwellers bore no resemblance to that of members of the same language groups who lived in Westernised cities, bereft of their ethnic heritage.)

To reach the hospital, patients and their *gardiens* had to trespass beyond their traditional land boundaries, traversing inhospitable, unfamiliar terrain, mainly over water, a danger-ridden distance from their home villages. Schweitzer built, at some distance from each other,

rays were the first to reveal the male parasite, and that it was to be found in an area of the body where it wasn't known to have existed. (*South African Medical Journal,* Dec.1959, pp.1094-5).

separate accommodations for patients of the warring groups.[29]

Clara Urquhart, who made several trips to see Schweitzer in Lambaréné, gives her memorable description of the hospital compound:

> ... A stranger arriving there unprepared could be forgiven for imagining that he had stumbled on Noah's Ark. The setting of river and swamp and jungle is certainly suitably primordial. . . Human beings and animals cross each other's paths all through the day. Under a tree in a fenced-off area live Schweitzer's antelopes; a tiny baby antelope which has to be fed from a bottle lives in one of the nurses' rooms; Parsifal the doctor's pelican, is to be found perched on a beam which runs across the square;[30] the porcupines are centrally placed, and the chimpanzee is fed on the balcony which overlooks the square and which houses dogs, cats, parrots, and other birds. Penelope, the gorilla, not only has a balcony all to herself, but she has too an African nursemaid all to herself. . .[31] The wild pigs are housed near the domestic breed of the same species; and the hens and the goats are literally all over the place all of the time." [32]

For all the critics' comments about a "lack of hygiene" at the hospital, when the statistics were examined, the low mortality rate turned out to be as good as any hospital in

---

[29] A 1950s demographic and ethnographic study of urbanisation in the country indicates that in the several administrative regions in and around Lambaréné, there was almost no movement – only 1% – of members of ethnic groups emigrating from one area to another. Marcel Soret, *Démographie et problèmes urbains en A.E.F.* (*Mémoires de l'institut d'études centralafricaines*, 1954).

[30] Parsifal, Lohengrin and Tristan were Schweitzer's pet pelicans.

[31] An infant ape behaves much like a human child until it reaches toddler age. My father was at Lambaréné when Penelope's future celebrity was set in train (see Part II below).

[32] Urquhart (1957), p.9.

Europe. Schweitzer was well-known to be a perfectionist. Several surgeons remarked on his meticulous attention to detail when he was operating himself.[33] He employed top-rate doctors from around the world and had a turn-over of the best medical people selected to volunteer for short periods. In the early 1960s the mortality rate was 1.17% – less that the average in Europe. In 2010, in the USA, it was 2.5%.

Admittedly, it is misleading to compare the statistics. A vocal critic, Dr George Cohen, for instance, told me that Schweitzer was "a bad doctor" – because if a patient was very old or terminally ill, he advised only conservative treatment. Dr Goldwyn was not reassured by the hospital's record of anaesthetic errors. But even if the impressive statistics reflect only the category of cases accepted, the fact remains that the Lambaréné standards were high and the mortality rates low.

ๆ๛

In the staff's living quarters, Schweitzer paid particular attention to the kitchen, anxious that nobody get ill from the food or the water in the compound.[34] The similarity is striking: Schweitzer was as anxious about people getting

---

[33] Goldwyn (12 November 1960) reported that he was a "slow, meticulous surgeon". Schweitzer stopped operating in 1950, when he was 75.

[34] In 1933, well-wishers in Alsace collected money to buy and send a refrigerator for the kitchen. It must have been the fairly new-fangled model recently on the market, powered by gas and liquid chemicals (that emanated CFCs, a danger still then undiscovered). It was an extraordinarily inappropriate gift to send to Schweitzer of all people, unless they were trying to make a point about at least some new inventions being useful. Perhaps the gift went to the house in Günsbach.

ill for those reasons as were his jungle hunter-gatherer neighbours. He knew how awful the consequences could be. In the last years of World War I, he had been afflicted with dysentery when he and his wife were in a French concentration camp. Later bowel complications necessitated several operations. His suffering was so extreme that, around 1920, it led to his developing a philosophical thesis about what he called "the brotherhood of the mark of pain". He concluded that an individual who has suffered and then been relieved of his suffering thenceforth has a moral obligation to help alleviate the suffering of others.

Schweitzer's anxiety about staff members becoming ill from food or water explains his disgruntlement every time one of them went to Lambaréné town. His real concern was that a meal there, where kitchens were not subject to his own strict regulations and where the water might not be boiled routinely, might result in a worker being laid off sick. This was an inconvenience that could be life-threatening – particularly to the patients, who would be without that staff member's expert attention.[35]

In the hospital kitchen, the production of each meal was overseen by a supervisor following Schweitzer's instructions. The kitchen staff wore rubber gloves. All

---

[35] Similarly, Schweitzer, ever the rationalist, insisted on Lambaréné staff and visitors wearing hats at all times, preferably pith helmets. The reason was to protect against sunstroke, or concussion, or mere unpleasantness as a result of what might fall out of the jungle's canopy. When his daughter re-connected with her father at the end of his life and went to work there, she refused to obey his silly rule about hats. It was the 1960s and everyone knew that pith helmets represented the decorative uniform of racist colonisers. Her defiant assertion of academic etiquette over his rationality nicely encapsulates the moral war that he waged his entire life.

water was boiled and all animal products were well cooked. Fruit and vegetables – from the large hospital orchards – were soaked in disinfectant before being washed in boiled water.

The dining table could accommodate thirty people. Schweitzer always sat facing the entrance to the room, in the middle of the table, not at the head, attended on either side by his long-term aides, Emma Haussknecht, Mathilde Kottmann or Ali Silver. The familiar, European, formal ritual of the meal contrasted sharply with the battle between artifice and nature outside the dining room. First there was prayer and thanksgiving. Then – and reports contradict each other – there was anything ranging from nervous silence to sparkling conversation. The table was always covered with a spotless table cloth. There was silver cutlery, and crockery brought from Europe. Aside from the occasional menu including crocodile or manioc, mainly the glassware, usually small, durable pickling jars, gave the game away.

৵৽৹

Schweitzer may have run away to Africa to escape European amorality but if he harboured any romantic fantasies about it being different in Africa, he was soon brought down to earth. Immediately, he had to accommodate himself to the independent spirit of the local people, their simultaneous resentment of and interest in foreigners, their indifference to the plight of someone not of their own ethnic group, their reluctance to be persuaded into paid labour and their disregard of contracts when they were. There were constant petty thefts, not always driven by desperation. For instance, his laboriously annotated Bach score disappeared forever from his room, filched by someone who had never seen a musical keyboard. There were also serious, costly deceptions, such as when he was sold hardwood that turned out to be softwood. He laughed, bitterly, about the large bunch of keys that always hung from his belt.

At the same time as Schweitzer reluctantly played the policeman, every so often he confused his staff by waiving his own rules. He allowed a known thief to return to the compound after he had been caught red-handed and had been roundly excluded by everyone, including the patients. Perhaps that is what forgiveness looks like.

In another example of Schweitzer's changeability, he had a soft spot for a particular disinhibited psychotic woman who perhaps suffered from severe Wernicke's dysphasia. For years, at unpredictable intervals, she would wander into the compound, disrupting the peace and scandalising visitors with her antics. He gave her the run of the place and appeared to have long, intense conversations with her – even though she spoke a language entirely of her own invention.

As in any conventional hospital, there was the necessity of maintaining a sharply defined, professional distance between staff and patients, not forgetting that they all lived in the same village. Transgressions of boundaries had to be kept vivid rather than politely subterranean. In one moving example, the visiting surgeon Dr Edgar Berman's wife, Phoebe, who had been helping in the infant ward, became attached to a particular orphaned baby. She asked Schweitzer if they could adopt the baby and take it back to America. Schweitzer refused, carefully explaining that the baby's villagers would want the child returned to them when it was well.[36]

---

[36] Edgar Berman, *In Africa with Schweitzer* (Harper and Row, 1986).

Another example of the professional struggle to find the boundary line between patient and carer, stars young Trudi Bochsler, who was in charge of the new leprosarium. She was notorious for her stand-up rows with Schweitzer, defending her demands for the special entitlements of "her lepers". (My father mentions his concern that she could catch leprosy, so closely did she work with the lepers.)

It still happened that attachment to patients led to their doctors' and nurses' heartache when those patients could not be saved. Many people, including my father on the occasion of the death of Schweitzer's wife, have written about Schweitzer's extreme lack of sentimentality. He never wore his heart on his sleeve, one might say. Nevertheless, there are reports of times when he had to isolate himself for a while after a patient died in order to deal with his distress.

Clara Urquhart put it thus:

> . . . if one goes to the Schweitzer hospital in good faith, if one discards all superficial bases of evaluation, if one remains there long enough to become aware that the doctor's dimensions are wider and deeper than those of the great majority, then everything one sees and experiences falls into place, like so many pawns in an expertly worked-out game of chess.[37]

---

[37] Urquhart (1957), p.21.

4

Women at Lambaréné

IN 1924 Noel Gillespie helped out as general factotum until he returned to university in August that year. The young Alsatian Dr Viktor Nessman arrived, staying until 1926. (He returned to France and in 1944 was killed by the Gestapo.) A steady stream of extraordinary people followed. There were large numbers of unchronicled transitory volunteers, such as my father, some of whom were already, or were to become, eminent in their professions elsewhere. Aside from these, over the fifty years, more than two hundred employees are recorded as having played substantial residential roles. Amongst them were several women who became eminently identified with Schweitzer's mission.

Mathilde Kottmann
The first medical assistant to arrive in Lambaréné, in July 1924, was a young Alsatian woman from Colmar, Mathilde Kottmann (1897-1973). She had first offered to volunteer in 1923 when she was a newly qualified midwife. Schweitzer said he had accepted her because she knew "how to be silent". With some other women there, she became synonymous with the hospital's long-term achievements. She never married and was at his side to the very end.

Ali Silver

At the end of 1947, Sister Ali (also called Almut or Alida) Silver arrived from Holland. Formerly with the Dutch Red Cross, she, too, became one of Schweitzer's most trusted colleagues. He told Clara Urquhart that Ali Silver was "an angel straight from Heaven".[38] Multilingual, she helped both as a nurse and as secretary, administrator and translator. In 1967, she established the main Schweitzer archives in Günsbach. She was the usual interpreter of English speakers' conversations with Schweitzer.

In his journal my father mentions Mathilde Kottmann and Ali Silver as comprising, with Schweitzer, the "big three". Ali Silver's politically poignant letter to my father in 1964 ends this book.

Emma Haussknecht

Another important woman in Schweitzer's life was another Alsatian, Emma Haussknecht (1895-1956). She also never married. She arrived a year after Mathilde Kottmann, on 10 October 1925, and worked there as his administrator until just before her unexpected death on 1 June 1956. Schweitzer was shattered. He placed her grave near a path he often walked along, and when his wife passed away a year later, he buried her ashes next to Emma Haussknecht's. He made his own coffin the year before he died and his own grave was the third on that plot.

---

[38] Urquhart (1957), p.26. Alida Silver (1914-1987) worked at the hospital during the following periods: 20 October 1947 - 16 May 1951, 12 December 1951 - 19 May 1954, 12 January 1955 - July 1966, September 1966 - April 1967. Thereafter she worked at the Schweitzer house in Günsbach. Her ashes are buried at Lambaréné, marked by the eighth cross.

Emmy Martin

Emmy Martin (1882- ?) played a central role in Schweitzer's life, so much so that some referred to her as his second wife. She too was Alsatian, a pastor's widow who began doing secretarial work for him as early as 1919 when he was working on the two volumes now known as *Philosophy and Civilization*. She came out to Lambaréné in 1925 and she was with him to the end. In later years, she was his chief administrator in Europe, and kept house for him at the hospital's offices that he built in 1929-1930 in his home town of Günsbach. It served as his base when he toured Europe and was used by his guests and by hospital workers on furlough. It is now a museum and archive.

Lilian Rigby

In the 1920s, when Schweitzer started life anew without his wife, he had another long and close association with a woman of whom Hélène was openly jealous. She was Mrs Charles E.B. Russell (1875-1949), a widow, of Scottish ancestry.[39] Of all the women who played an important role in his life, Lilian Rigby, nicknamed "Madame Canada" by staff at Lambaréné, is

---

[39] Aside from her academic publications she also wrote a popular book, *My Monkey Friends* (1938), based on her Lambaréné experiences. At the end of her life she wrote a book, published posthumously, honouring her brilliant professor at Queen's College, *John Adam Cramb* (1950). Separately, and inexplicably, her father appears as a fantasy character in Mark Hodder's steampunk novel, *The Rise of the Automated Aristocrats* (2015). Lilian Rigby is not the "Mrs Charles Russell" painted by John Singer Sargent in 1900. This was Adah Williams, wife of the lawyer who helped Queensbury win his case against Oscar Wilde.

the least mentioned in the literature. She asked that her association with Schweitzer not be described. For nineteen years, between 1927 and 1946, she was categorised in the hospital records as simply *aide de partout*.

Lilian Rigby had been educated at Queen's College in Harley Street, London, a rather progressive girls' day school founded in 1848. It still exists. Although she was only ten when her father died, she may already have acquired a sense of Africa before she arrived in Lambaréné: her father was Major-General Christopher Palmer Rigby (1820-1885) of the Indian Staff Corps, who had been posted in India and East Africa. He was Zanzibar's British Consul from 1858 to 1861. In 1935 she published his papers, demonstrating his work as an anti-slavery activist and as a gifted linguist.

Lilian Rigby married Charles E. B. Russell (1866-1917). They worked together in indigent areas of Manchester, researching and writing about working class life, especially about disaffected boys, and women in prison. From 1913 Charles E. B. Russell was employed by the Home Office as Chief Inspector of Reformatory and Industrial Schools. He died suddenly of heart trouble on 17 April 1917, his 51st birthday.

When she first arrived in Lambaréné ten years later, in 1927, both she and Schweitzer were 52. She remained involved with the hospital for the next eighteen years, until 1945 or 1946, when she was seventy, three years before she died. Possibly she was there when Hélène, having crossed the war-torn oceans in a Portuguese ship, made a dramatic and unexpected appearance at the Adoninalongo landing late one night in August 1941.

In the early 1930s Lilian Rigby took the first film footage of Schweitzer that Jerome Hill and Erica

Anderson later used in their documentary about him. She translated into English his *Indian Thought and its Development* (1936) and *From My African Notebook* (1938) and also wrote her own, impressive, summary of Schweitzer's philosophical work, *The Path to Reconstruction* (1943).

It was Lilian Rigby, with Emma Haussknecht, who supervised forest clearance in order to extend the orchard and vegetable gardens. By the time of her last departure from Lambaréné, the orchard was the largest in the country.

Anna Wildikann

Another woman whose name is connected with Schweitzer's is Dr Anna Wildikann (1901-1987). She was originally from Riga and had first volunteered to work with him after hearing him speak when he toured Europe in the early 1930s. She was a surgeon at his hospital from 18 May 1935 to 10 September 1937, and at intervals between 8 January 1940 and 29 December 1945.

On one of Schweitzer's birthdays, she gave him a book of photographs she had taken of Parsifal, his favourite pet pelican. During World War II, she managed to get from Lambaréné to Jerusalem to have an operation at the Hadassah Hospital and hoped to stay in the country once she was well. The British Mandate authorities refused her permission to remain. She returned to Lambaréné, raised funds to buy leave to remain and returned as a volunteer doctor at a British internment camp for Holocaust survivors. (Her sister had been murdered in the Holocaust.) After the British withdrew, she worked at Hadassah Hospital.

Schweitzer realised she would need to buy a car. He quickly wrote the children's book, *The Story of My*

Pelican, to accompany the photographs she had taken, and gifted the royalties of its publication to her. They kept in touch. Dr Wildikann visited Schweitzer whenever he was in Europe, including when he received the Nobel Peace Prize in Oslo. In the book, Schweitzer tells the story from Parsifal's point of view. The bird remarks of Schweitzer, "I found it very strange that such a good man could grumble such a lot." In real life, later, Parsifal was wounded by a hunter's gun-shot and Schweitzer, typically unsentimental, suspended his "reverence for life" while he put the bird out of its misery, a brutal ending that didn't feature in the children's book.

Clara Urquhart

Clara Urquhart (1907-1986), the so-called "steel heiress", was much more than this. She was a South African intellectual, a humanitarian fixer, facilitator, radical political activist and philanthropist. During and after World War II, she worked for UNRRA in Geneva and with the Red Cross department for prisoners of war in South Africa. Later, her various para-political activities, if examined, might go some way towards illuminating the misty world of backstage politics during the eventful post-war period.

Curiously, while her name crops up all over the place, as yet there appears to be no biography of Clara Urquhart (née Rosenberg) and information about her personal life is hard to find. In 1926, she married Monty Baranov (1895-1928). He died two years later. She married again and in 1944 divorced her second husband. She had no children.

A staunch supporter of Schweitzer's philosophy and practice, she regularly visited Lambaréné, facilitating the visits of influential guests, volunteer workers and donors.[40]

My father must have known Clara Urquhart. He was an obvious candidate in the medical community to be invited to volunteer at Lambaréné but he was also a long-standing friend of Muriel Balkin who, I discovered while doing this research, was Clara Urquhart's niece. It was through Urquhart that several people mentioned in this book came to Lambaréné, such as Dr Frank Catchpool in London, Norman Cousins in New York, and Ruth Dayan in Tel Aviv. Schweitzer's most well-respected biographer, the white Ugandan James Brabazon, said that he began to write his book thanks to Clara Urquhart's encouragement.

Early in 1957 Urquhart brought American author and journalist Norman Cousins to Lambaréné. Since 1942, Cousins had been editor-in-chief of New York's *Saturday Review*.[41] He and Schweitzer had been in correspondence and now he wanted to persuade the famously apolitical[42]

---

[40] Clara Urquhart's introductions to Schweitzer were not always in Lambaréné. Erich Fromm is a good example. She had a long friendship with the psychoanalyst, and their intense correspondence is extant, as is Schweitzer's with Fromm. See the biography by Lawrence J. Friedman, *The Lives of Erich Fromm: Love's Prophet* (Columbia U.P., 2013).

[41] Cousins suffered from a disease of the connective tissue which left him in constant pain. He wrote extensively about new discoveries in the relationship between what we eat – the body's biochemistry – and emotional states.

[42] Dr George Cohen was still rancorous fifty-eight years after the event when he told me that he'd asked Schweitzer why he had never condemned Nazi atrocities and Schweitzer would not answer him. Clara Urquhart, in her 1957 book about Lambaréné, was equally disturbed by Schweitzer's silence on the subject. My own interpretation is that the question itself, transparently testing, is problematic, if not an affront to Schweitzer. It ignores his commitment to action rather than words and also his *raison d'être,* his philosophy of "reverence

doctor to put his name to the growing nuclear disarmament lobby in which Cousins was increasingly involved.

At the same time as Clara Urquhart was assisting the growing anti-nuclear protest, she was lobbying, successfully, for Albert Luthuli to receive the Nobel Peace Prize for his advocacy of non-violent resistance to racial discrimination in South Africa. Luthuli was president of the African National Congress (ANC), the largest South African liberation party. Along with other organisations opposing the Nationalist government, it was banned in South Africa until 2 February 1990. The Nobel Peace Prize was awarded to Luthuli in 1960.

Erica Anderson

Another woman whose name is associated closely with Schweitzer's later life, was photographer Erica Anderson (1914-1976). In November 1957, a few months after Hélène's death, the documentary film, *Albert Schweitzer* was released. It was directed by the philanthropist Jerome Hill with cinematography by Erica Anderson.

During the several years that it took to make the film, and for the years until his death, she and Schweitzer maintained a close friendship both in Lambaréné and on his visits to Europe.[43] The documentary went on to win an Oscar. Although its tone is hagiographic, it is historically accurate, intelligently made, and at the time of writing this, is perhaps the only watchable film about Schweitzer.

---

for life". The short answer is to the effect, "Of course he condemned it. How can you even ask? Consider how he lived his life."

[43] Erica Anderson, *The Schweitzer Album: a portrait in words and pictures* (Harper, 1965).

In our little detour from prominent women in Schweitzer's life to films about him, let us note that in 1969 Henry Fonda voiced over "a new one hour color TV Special" by Warner Bros. It was entitled *The Legacy of Albert Schweitzer*. The advertising poster reads: "Henry Fonda narrates the incredible story of Albert Schweitzer and the man he inspired to fulfil his legacy, Dr Walter Munz". It was aired only once on American television. Supposedly there is a deteriorating copy in the archives of Fonda's daughter, Jane, but she has not responded to enquiries about it. Perhaps the reason for the film's disappearance has no purport; or perhaps there were internal politics at play.

Dr Munz remained on the board of the umbrella organisation, AISL, for years after he left Lambaréné but history has more or less expunged mention of him as heir to Schweitzer's domain. Nearing death, Schweitzer chose him to be medical director with Schweitzer's daughter, Rhena, as administrative director.

Rhena Schweitzer had begun visiting the hospital after her mother's death. After her father's death, she took up a dominant position there, along with her American partner, Dr David C. Miller, whom she had met at the hospital and whom she later married. They were bent on modernisation. After five – surely gruelling – years, they left Lambaréné for Georgia, America and elsewhere. The hospital did not survive the "improvements".

Implicit in Schweitzer's philosophy was that reverence for life requires keeping things on a human scale. The alternative is death.

ঙ্কৃ

Hélène Bresslau was always at pains to remind everyone that in 1913 she co-founded the Lambaréné hospital with her husband, and that thereafter it was not just one man's achievement but a woman's too, namely hers. It is truer to say that there were, undeniably, unsung heroines who made the difficult medical work possible but she was not, unfortunately, one of them. She contributed little compared to others, and there were many others, many more than the women I have mentioned above. There were several women in the early days before he was married who championed Schweitzer's project with ideas and funds, so that he – with Hélène Bresslau, it turned out – could make a first African assay.

The nature of Schweitzer's relationships with all these women is not exactly known. Edouard Nies-Berger (1903-2002) is the most notoriously outspoken but there is little corroboration elsewhere.[44] He tells the tale, for instance, of Hélène Bresslau walking in on "Madame Canada" kissing (*sic*) Schweitzer, that Bresslau despised the woman ever after and immediately sold off the expensive furniture that Lilian Rigby had bequeathed to Schweitzer on her death.

On a separate note, it is statistically probable that some of the many women who surrounded Schweitzer for years were in relationships not with him but with each other. In the ample literature about him, nobody mentions this interesting likelihood. The research has yet to be done.

---

[44] Edouard Nies-Berger, "Albert Schweitzer as I knew him" in *The Complete Organ series, no. 5* (Pendragon Press, 2002).

5

Straw Man

"Yes, I had success, but I paid for it.
I had to put up with people all my life,
especially in Lambaréné.
You do not know what a terrible life I have had."
Schweitzer quoted in Nies-Berger (2002), p. 83.

THE motif of knocking down a straw man was especially common in the reporting on Schweitzer from around 1960 when, as we shall see, there was a confluence of disparate external agencies that wanted to diminish his moral standing.

Schweitzer never set out to be either a saint on the one hand or a threat to Western civilisation on the other, both of which he was held to be at different times. Some people needed to put him on a pedestal and others, or even the same people, needed afterwards to knock him down. Because *in extremis* we fear, hate and envy power, we may be driven to cast down idols without much preliminary enquiry into what those idols represent, without thought about who elevated them in the first place: perhaps ourselves.

Having looked into Schweitzer's life with an ample sufficiency of post-millennial scepticism, my conclusion is that aspersions cast upon him are overplayed. The assorted circumstances that prompt the aspersions are wonderfully revealing of the critics themselves, the *zeitgeist*, and the ever-present difficulty of doing good.

Schweitzer couldn't bear what we would call political correctness as mouthed by do-gooders, including journalists, who had no sincere respect for others' very different ways of life. His apparent eccentricity, his outbursts of unsaintly short temper, his impatience with naive idealists – as well as racists – who perforce couldn't see through his wicked baiting of them, led to his being an easy target.

His worst critics didn't stay in Lambaréné for long enough to understand what it was he was really doing there and why. They didn't seem to have read his books, aside perhaps from the light, anecdotal ones intended to raise money for the hospital. They didn't grasp that his project was the result of a rational examination of the canon of moral philosophy from both the East and the West. Meanwhile, any convincing disagreement with him needed to be argued on equally erudite grounds.

By 1960, with the advent of commercial air-travel, it was much easier to visit Lambaréné than it had ever been before. A constant flow of sight-seeing visitors wanted the novelty of a pirogue ride through breath-taking, surreal water-scapes followed by a glimpse of the Nobel laureate in his jungle lair. Dr Weissberg was once called upon to provide some of his – of course empty – government hospital beds for a coach-size group of Scandinavians who clambered on to Schweitzer's dock, assuming that they would be led to hotel rooms.

Members of the transient white tourist tribe often didn't see that a local person wanted to do things his or her own way, perhaps taking here and there something of what the whites offered, perhaps not. Nobody wanted the whites to tell them how to live their lives. White critics, including a few black academics overseas, sometimes said that Schweitzer should have imported Western ways instead of replicating a native village and calling it a hospital. They had failed to notice that his aim was to provide relief from physical pain and suffering, an aim that had nothing to do with requiring local people to live like white people.

Publications about him often assume his intentionality at every turn. They refer to his supposed aim to promote an ideology, or his failure to do so. They mention the African medical schools he should have established, or the African languages he should have learnt to speak, or the Indian religions he should not have studied, and so on. He always said of himself that he'd made it up as he went along: his carefully considered values guided his actions according to each problem as it arose.[45]

At the time, the cultural divide between foreign doctor and local patient was immense. Today, contemplation of that historical separation can make us feel guilty and also confused. Most of the world has been Americanised. Just about every young person wants the privileges and appliances that the West has to offer – a rectangular home, mod-cons, air-con, social media devices, junk-food, junk-drink, the international uniform of tee-shirts, jeans and trainers. Provision of such assets has been elevated to the benchmark of every new government's minimal obligation. Should surviving ancient cultures be protected or should they be helped to die out?

There is no record of a member of one of the local ethnic groups ever trying to enter Schweitzer's white world and then being or even feeling rejected. Difficult as

---

[45] For an even-handed academic overview of Schweitzer's philosophical writings, see Predrag Cicovacki (ed.), *Albert Schweitzer's Ethical Vision: A Sourcebook* (O.U.P, 2009).

it was for foreign visitors to believe then, or perhaps for Western readers to believe now, there was nothing especially attractive about anything the whites' compound or the foreign staff had to offer. Admittedly, there was the enviable easy access to staple food but the attraction was not so great as to warrant surrendering one's entire culture for that ease. Another attraction was the white doctor's capacity to provide relief from aspects of some illnesses that local sorcerer-healers could not alleviate. Then again, the whites were ignorant of the most important aspects of illness, namely the machinations of the spirit world that originate problems in the body.

Amongst the visitors and volunteer staff, there was also sometimes a clash between American and European cultural values, as fluid and imprecise as these were. Back in the 1950s there was a difference between how the middle classes in America were living, with their cars, their modern kitchens and their colour coordinated bathrooms, compared to the average family household in Europe. Post-war Europe was utterly impoverished and was wholly dependent on American aid and American anxiety that if it didn't help, Russia would step in.

American urban culture bore little resemblance to that of most Europeans'. In the early 1960s, most Europeans had not been to secondary school, let alone university. Most Europeans could not afford dishwashers or washing machines, and anyway the electricity grids would not have been large enough to drive them *en masse*. If households were affluent enough to own a television set, they watched it only for a few hours a week. The outdoor toilet was only just beginning to gravitate towards the back wall of the house.

In the early 1960s, America's European counterparts had barely dragged themselves out of the financial penury of World War II. Americans, discovering that they were citizens of the richest and most powerful nation on earth, overflowed with generosity. They wanted everyone to be as lucky as they were and to live as they did. They were unaware that their concern and sympathy was often patronising, insulting.

Whatever their background, European or American, to the left or to the right, Schweitzer's severest critics had in common their outrage at his minimal disruption of the existing way of life. How could it be a good thing for a white man to go to Africa and not disseminate Western culture? It had to be wrong, even bad, that his hospital deliberately replicated, as far as possible, the patients' village life.

The musician and film-maker, the late Sam Zebba (1924-2016), mentioned in his 2009 blog that when he was a prize-winning graduate in the early 1950s, he was inspired to make a film about Schweitzer. As a teenager visiting his hospitalised mother in Israel, he had met a woman sharing her ward, who happened to be one of Schweitzer's doctors, Dr Anna Wildikann. She was to become his surrogate mother, mentor, and friend. Back in New York and eager to make the film, Zebba contacted the Albert Schweitzer Fellowship. He was surprised by the reluctance of the organisation to facilitate documentation of the hospital. The quiet explanation was that the hospital was "antiquated" and that Schweitzer's "legendary ethic of 'Reverence for Life'... allowed chickens and stray monkeys to roam freely through the wards. If people saw this the Fellowship feared donations would cease."[46]

---

[46] http://esra-magazine.com/blog/post/anna-and-i

The doctor who took over from Dr Weissberg at the government hospital in Lambaréné town, is another example of someone unable to appreciate the discrepancy between his own expectations and Schweitzer's intentions. For two years, between 1963-1966, Dr André Audoynaud ran the provincial hospital, replacing Dr Weissberg. Forty years after Schweitzer's death, Audoynaud published a rant querying the status that had been accorded *le grand docteur*. Audoynaud claimed that the man had merely built a shanty-town on the other side of the river and had offered poor medical services compared to what was on offer at the government hospital.

Much of Audoynaud's claim may be true. Curiously, he seems not to have asked himself why, despite that being the case, Schweitzer's "shanty-town" continued to attract an annually increasing number of patients – so many, in fact, that the infrastructure couldn't cope with the influx. In contrast, there was the hardly patronised "modern" hospital of which Audoynaud had been given charge for a couple of years.

More striking than his objections to Schweitzer's "shanty-town" is his display of incomprehension about either Schweitzer's moral rationale or his practical problem-solving over the decades, that accounted for the apparently eccentric outcome. Audoynard made the same error as later "improvers" were to make. He did not recognise that Schweitzer's project, for all its failings, had a coherent philosophical and moral underpinning that manifestations of existing forms of government, such as the government hospital in Lambaréné town, could never share.

There were a handful of writers around 1960, notably the British James Cameron on the left and American Gerald Knight on the right, who, for different reasons, were impelled to try to sully Schweitzer's moral renown. Exposing an idol's feet of clay has the ring of serious investigative journalism. Besides, Lambaréné always made good copy because not only were there its exotic oddities, including the doctor himself, but at any one time a visitor was bound to bump into another visitor or even worker who was very famous or very rich or very brilliant or all three at once. If a journalist gained entry for a quick look, then a happy editor, remuneration, and prestige back home were guaranteed. Never mind that the condemnation affected the hospital's funding.

It turned out that right-wingers were superfluous to the task of bringing down Schweitzer. The left-wingers did it for them. By casting suspicion on Schweitzer's life-long struggle to alleviate physical suffering, by mocking his leaving a minimal Western footprint, left-wing and liberal writers fulfilled the intentions of the right-wing lobby.

Over the years, Schweitzer was accused of not being a good Christian, of having gone native, of being a racist, a white missionary, a Communist, a German spy, an emissary of Western colonialism, a utopian dreamer, a cold pragmatist. He was described as self-serving and as selfless, as a good doctor and a bad doctor, as kind and charming, and as rude and aggressive, as a brilliant musician, as a poor musician, a ground-breaking philosopher, a bad philosopher, as a throwback to Prussian imperialism and as a thinker ahead of his time.

Scrutiny of his far-away activities used to fill newspapers, magazines, libraries, the radio-waves, and documentary film. There have been a few feature films purporting to be biographical. One portrayed him as a crazed sadist, another as a flawed saint, a bit of a fool. There is a justified European compulsion to assuage past guilt but it is risible that funders of those curiosities paid for yet more re-writing of history in Africa when, as we shall see later, there are plenty of genuine atrocities to be interrogated on both sides of the racial divide.

There is a difference between racism, paternalism, condescension, thoughtlessness and ignorance. These days, since we have become hyper-vigilant about being politically correct, we find it difficult to distinguish between them. A person's skin colour *per se* did not prompt what could be construed either as Schweitzer's authoritarianism or else strong leadership. In a complimentary mood, his friend and colleague, Frederick Franck, described Schweitzer in a socialist vein: he resembled a traditional farmer who made the rules about how his land should be husbanded. He was "what in German is called a *'Groszbauer'* [a large-scale farmer] and his Hospital is his farm."[47] If he behaved as if he were in charge it was because the land was his responsibility and in point of fact, he *was* in charge.

Was he good? Was he bad? Schweitzer has been attributed with a range of contradictory qualities that reveal less about him than they do about the cultural imperatives driving the people doing the judging. Consider the following frequently cited example of an article by the legendary liberal journalist James Cameron.

Cameron made a quick visit to Lambaréné in 1953 and was so appalled by what, according to his standards, was

---

[47] Frederick Franck, *Days with Albert Schweitzer: a Lambaréné landscape* (1959; Greenwood, 1974). Moments in Graham Greene's novel *A Burnt Out Case* (1960) – something of a meditation on Schweitzer's moral position in Lambaréné – suggest his acquaintance with Franck's book.

general squalor, that he held back on publishing his impressions until many years had passed. He was shocked: not only was there no electricity or plumbing but Schweitzer did not socialise with the black people around him.[48]

Schweitzer told him, first, that no black doctor had ever volunteered to help at the hospital, and second, that he never would sit down at his table with an *indigène*. To Cameron's mind, this was evidence of Schweitzer's racism. Meanwhile, Schweitzer would have found Cameron's questions ridiculous, if not an affront. Cameron was transparently baiting him, aside from insulting his intelligence and his own life-long, thoughtful dedication to his task.

My hunch is that, like most other critics, Cameron had not read Schweitzer's philosophy books. His preconceptions of the doctor's views were based on remarks Schweitzer had made in his first fund-raising exercise. This was the slim, undemanding book he wrote about Lambaréné based on his first four years there from

---

[48] James Cameron (1911-1985), *Point of Departure* (1967; Oriel, 1985), pp. 152-174. The Scottish journalist of legendary stature is not to be confused with the Canadian film director (1954 -). Cameron is unaware that his article about Schweitzer has a visible crack down the middle. It starts with his original adulatory notes, made on his visit years before. Then he adds his reformulated critical material based on his supposition of the benefits of progress: another straw man attack. At the end, Cameron wonders whether Schweitzer was "pulling his leg" when Cameron interrogated him about his purportedly not wanting to share his dining table with an *indigène*. Cameron concludes that Schweitzer had *not* been joking. But - of course Schweitzer was winding him up! He was indicating the idiocy of Cameron's interrogation but if Cameron had had it in him to see the joke, he wouldn't have behaved idiotically in the first place.

1913. Since then his views and vocabulary had moved on with the times.

Schweitzer was familiar with the supposed anti-racist formula that was itself a racist slur. Rather than waste time propounding its objectionable components, he usually resorted to baiting his interrogator in turn with his own fearless contrariness. Schweitzer often expressed his exasperation with sharp, coded humour, sending people up without their knowing it. It is the only ungodly behaviour one detects in him, invariably, one must admit, justifiable. One might call it cruelly witty were it not that he was not point-scoring. Indeed, he must have known he would probably lose points. And he did. The press made a meal of it but he did not care.

With Cameron's beady investigative journalist's eye on him, it probably didn't help that Schweitzer's bedside manner with patients could be testy. His patients were black. Schweitzer would have been incentivised to provoke Cameron. Particularly annoying would have been Cameron's oblivious disrespect of those so-called *indigènes* about whom he pretended to be concerned. Schweitzer must have asked, silently, of course, why the journalist didn't object rather to their not extending to Cameron an invitation to dine. And, for that matter, did Cameron really suppose that the local people were longing for the pleasure of dining with the doctor? For one thing, they weren't so stupid as to eat food made by an unknown hand in a distant kitchen.

Cameron was a well-meaning man of his times but his assumption that Schweitzer was withholding something precious from the poor black person contains within it a mote of Eurocentrism, even racism, so large that it was a wonder he was not blinded by it. The journalist 's attempt to catch out Schweitzer (and he would be followed by others) presumed that the white way was superior to the black way and should be benevolently bestowed upon local people.

Should one presume that Schweitzer's familiar reticence – one could never say of him, he "doth protest too much" – signalled that he ignored what a few, loud voices said behind his back? Was he untouched by the self-serving attacks upon his integrity? One day he called a great gathering of all the patients and the staff at the hospital. He asked if they wanted him to close the hospital and go away. Everyone was alarmed by his very question. They shouted that he must stay.

ॐ

Somebody who exhibited profound understanding of Schweitzer's enterprise was the American philanthropist, Lawrence Gussman, Chair and CEO of Stein Hall, Inc. in the years 1953 to 1971. Gussman and his wife, Kaye, first became interested in Schweitzer after they visited Johannesburg on business at the end of 1956 and were offered flights to Lambaréné. They travelled with the medical volunteers Dr Sydney Joel-Cohen and Dr Bobby Roberts.

The Gussmans returned several times before Schweitzer's death in 1965. In 1971, when Schweitzer's daughter Rhena gave up running the hospital and returned to America, things had started to go awry. Gussman stepped in to rescue the situation in a business-like way, taking the reins from afar as President of the AISL. He divided it into two completely separate branches, one that dealt with the local funding and running of the Lambaréné hospital on a day-to-day basis and the other that managed funds and projects abroad, perpetuating Schweitzer's philosophy. Like the unfortunate new-born twins of the Ogowe region, one seems to have been destined to die.

Gussman's work had been a rescue mission. By 1974 the hospital's resources were disappearing. The Gabon government tried to help plug the gap. Between 1976 and 1981 the original Lambaréné hospital was a tourist site and a large new concrete complex went up in its stead, using its name. It included a modern hospital with large maternity and dental care departments, staff accommodation, administrative offices, a police department, and government health services. Before long, funds, wages, equipment, provisions, staff and managers began to evaporate. As we noted earlier, by 2016 there were reports that the functioning of the Albert Schweitzer Hospital at Lambaréné had slowed down or stopped. In America and Europe the bona fide charities operating in Schweitzer's name remain highly active.

6

The Fog of Philanthropy

IN 1913 when he first went to Africa with his wife, he a newly qualified doctor and she a barely qualified nurse, Schweitzer never guessed that fifty years later he would still need to be extending the hospital compound to cater for the jungle-dwellers' ever-growing demand for his medical services. A regular injection of funds from abroad was needed to pay for the ongoing building and maintenance, and to cater for the swelling numbers of visiting doctors, administrators, assistants and tourists.

Schweitzer needed impeccable credentials for the hospital to receive the charitable donations on which its continuation depended. During his tours around Europe and, in 1949, on his single visit to America,[49] audiences sampled his charm as well as his musical and story-telling talents. Despite having to use interpreters, he conveyed his moral integrity, his brilliance and his modesty. Donors trusted that with him their money would be properly spent.

---

[49] The Boston-based Albert Schweitzer Fellowship, established ten years earlier, helped arrange Schweitzer's visit (including some touring) to give his lecture on Goethe at the International Goethe Convocation in Aspen, in July 1949. The talk was recorded for posterity using new technology: two 78 rpm vinyl records. He delivered the speech in German and Thornton Wilder translated it.

Aside from a donor's tax benefits and philanthropy's elevation of a person's social standing, there is also that tacit contract where the donor makes reparation for some feelings of guilt, or guilt by association. Schweitzer did not disparage a penitential impulse. He himself admitted that he had been assuaging his guilt in starting the hospital in the first place. He said that he had had a life of European privilege, built on imperial and colonial exploitation. The concept of privilege is relative: his father had been a village pastor of modest income. Nevertheless, compared to other village boys, young Albert understood that he had been granted, arbitrarily, an advantage.

There were and still are hundreds of lay missionaries all over the world doing good work in obscure and dangerous places. We've never heard of them. The difference with Schweitzer's project was that he led it from the front, mucking in himself at every turn, attending to every detail. Busy in his remote bailiwick, he retained the allure of a well-connected man of integrity, drawing towards him brilliant, equally well-connected people from the hub of global affairs. They were active in the world while he, needing their exteriority, largely kept his own distance from it. The force of his presence generated an atmosphere that surrounded the location. It was a climate of values shared by a community of like-minded thinkers, each striving to contribute as best they could. Most visitors sensed the benevolent undercurrent and commented on it, even someone as resistant as Ruth Dayan, as we shall see later.

Lambaréné during Schweitzer's long life-time would seem to have been the most unlikely international social hub but that is what it became. Indirectly, that is what kept it going, and not only financially. The

70

philanthropists, usually famous and newsworthy themselves, sometimes visited Lambaréné, especially in the years after Schweitzer won the Nobel Peace Prize in 1952. Journalists trailed in their wake, snapping up marketable titbits, from gossip to the gravely political.

His wife accused him of being attention-seeking. She did not acknowledge that it was only by drawing attention to his project, by exploiting his personality and his philosophy, that he could encourage charitable contributions to support the hospital – and also, rather well, his wife and daughter. For him it was all of a piece, a social ecosystem, what Urquhart called "an expertly worked-out game of chess".[50] The imputation of a game may be misleading but not so the suggestion that at any one time a great mind was calculating a *good* outcome from countless small moves.

From the time of Schweitzer's return to Lambaréné in 1924, over two hundred members of staff are on record as having come from abroad to help. In addition to this number, there were many more, volunteers such as my father, who visited for brief periods, from a few days to a few months. Of them there is no single record. They came and went and came back again, meeting anew in changing configurations, forming relationships with each other that continued in other countries, their common experience in Lambaréné, the moral atmosphere, marking the locus of intense connection. The aura of ethical enterprise illuminated powerful memories of their time there, much as happens to support workers in a war zone. Their personal associations formed a strong, invisible net of interlocking narratives that held up the massive weight of the medical enterprise. Schweitzer could not possibly

---

[50] Urquhart (1957), p.21.

have foreseen it or planned it but his hospital's longevity much depended on the ever-widening web of friendships for which he was the catalyst.

When people left Lambaréné, the experience became part of their self-description. The same individuals became automatic emissaries for raising funds to keep the hospital going. Lawrence Gussman is a vivid example. He was randomly offered a flight to Lambaréné in 1957 and less than twenty years later he was at its international organisational helm. Along the way, he had also become a world expert on the art of central Africa.

Romantic relationships also contributed towards the cohesiveness of the whole enterprise. The place was a figurative, and of course also literal, hot-house, an anchored ark in more ways than one. In its confines, there were ship-board romances, followed by *ersatz* or actual marriages and divorces. Sometimes the intensity of the connection was a little too much for others to take, let alone the protagonists. Doctors Edgar Berman and Frederick Franck separately both write about sound carrying between rooms because of the mesh screen walls. While during the day it seemed that most workers were single, at night one was as likely to overhear a couple's ablutions as to overhear their arguments or their sexual intercourse.

Most of the time, Schweitzer kept away from contentions between couples unless a serious turn required his Solomon-esque verdict. We know that at least once he had to judge whether or not an abortion would be performed under his auspices when a member of staff became pregnant in inauspicious circumstances.

While the intrusion of interpersonal spats was annoying in the workplace (my father and separately Dr Robert Goldwyn remark on this), they were an ingredient in the glue of fealty. Transitory Lambaréné volunteers became unstated life-members of a group bound together by their shared memories, the hard work, the heat, their moral and medical triumphs, and also their passionate disagreements.

An invisible net supported the fame and reach of the medical "shanty-town", with Schweitzer as inadvertent precipitant. Sampling something of its complexity helps one to bring into focus the larger picture.

ॐ

In May 1957, my father refers to meeting Dr "Catchford" and assisting in his place in the operating theatre because "Catchford" is ill. He struggles with the strange surname: he means Dr John Francis "Frank" Catchpool (1925-2006), then thirty-two, an English Quaker whom Clara Urquhart had known in London. It was she who initially arranged for Catchpool to come to work with Schweitzer. He was there from 22 November 1956 to 1 September 1958 and again from 24 April to 16 November 1959.[51]

In 1959 Catchpool was back in Lambaréné after an eight-month break. He met Linus Pauling and his wife Ava Helen who were visiting for a week from 16 July. Pauling was soon so impressed with his new acquaintance that by 1960 he had appointed Catchpool to a research post at Cal Tech and then at the Pauling Institute.

Ava Helen Pauling's entry for 17 July 1959 reads: "Dr Catchpool is only 34. [It was his birthday the day before.]

---

[51] Norman Cousins describes meeting Catchpool in February 1957 when he arrived with Clara Urquhart. Bobby Roberts describes meeting him when he arrived from Johannesburg with Dr Joel-Cohen and the Gussmans.

Nurses from Holland, Switzerland, South Africa – one beautiful one from Mexico." One can't tell if the verbal association of Catchpool and the Mexican nurse is deliberate. She notes that Catchpool was grey-haired and looked ten years older, his face "lined with the care and anxiety he feels for these patients".

Catchpool's care and anxiety did not render him oblivious to the beautiful "Mexican nurse". She was Adriana Eller (b. 1933), the grand-daughter of the dictator and former President of Mexico, Plutarco Elias Calles. Catchpool soon married her and they had a son, Christopher. They divorced after a few years and she settled in California. During the Biafran War (1968-70), Catchpool worked amongst the Ibo, and afterwards in a remote Mexican village before moving to San Rafael, California in 1973. In 1974, he became clinic director at the Linus Pauling Institute in Menlo Park.

Adriana Eller became an art collector and an expert on the work of Miguel Covarrubias. By coincidence – as is required in the lost soap opera we have found – her thirty-nine year-long second marriage was to Thomas J. Williams, the widower of Nancy Guggenheim Draper (1915-1972). Nancy Guggenheim was the daughter of Harry Frank Guggenheim by his first marriage; his third, in 1939, was to Alicia Patterson. A couple of weeks after my father had left Lambaréné in 1957, Alicia Patterson arrived there, part of a group brought by Adlai Stevenson, the American Democratic presidential candidate who had recently lost to Eisenhower.

Visiting at the same time as the Paulings in 1959 was Schweitzer's daughter, Rhena. She had brought her oldest child from her first marriage, Christiane Eckert (later Engel), who was paying her first visit to Lambaréné. Christiane Eckert was already a gifted pianist and later qualified as a doctor. On 18 July 1959 Ava Helen Pauling wrote: "Very trying for everyone here. All the photographers, etc. Nurses and doctors incensed." The gathering of more than the usual quotient of famous people had attracted journalists, as often happened.

According to Ava Helen Pauling, the photographers who were plaguing the place were looking also for an heiress, one of the richest women in the world, who was rumoured to be volunteering at the hospital. Nobody seemed to be able to help them find her. (Perhaps, for a laugh, she posed part-time as one of them, as we shall see.) A journalist put his head round the kitchen door but saw only a tired looking woman peeling vegetables so he carried on looking elsewhere.

Olga Deterding (1926-1978) was thirty when she came to volunteer at the hospital in 1956. She was a daughter of one of the richest men in the world, Henri Deterding, the Dutch architect of the Shell oil company. She had suffered from mood swings and at least once attempted suicide. In her youth, she was described by Pat Cavendish O'Neil as "great fun but very scatty".[52] She found respite at Lambaréné. Probably my father unwittingly witnessed the developing relationship between her and Frank Catchpool back in mid-1957 but it's no surprise that he didn't put two and two together, or if he did, that he didn't think it was worth commenting on.

Catchpool and Olga Deterding were together later in London and visited America as a couple the following year, 1958. Dr Lawrence (Larry) Mellon had been inspired by Schweitzer to train as a doctor and follow in his footsteps. Uniquely, he followed literally. In 1956,

---

[52] Pat Cavendish O'Neil, *A Lion in the Bedroom* (Park Street Press, 2004), ch.48.

with his wife Gwen, Mellon opened his *Hôpital Albert Schweitzer Haiti*. On 10 December 1958, Mellon mentions in a letter to Schweitzer that Dr Catchpool and Olga Deterding visited the week before. They later returned to Lambaréné which must have been when Ava Helen Pauling wrote (23 July 1959): "Met Olga, photographer, who turns out to be Olga Deterding – owner of Shell!!! . . . Fond of Catchpool!!! She is a sallow-skinned, tall Englishwoman. Not much oomph, I think, but much, much money!!"

It would have been during this time that Catchpool formed an attachment to Adriana Eller, "the Mexican nurse", whose beauty Ava Helen Pauling remarked upon. Olga Deterding went back to London suffering from "a tropical disease". It was after this that Catchpool and Adriana Eller married.

The mature Olga Deterding was described as down-to-earth, intelligent, and the last of London's literary hostesses.[53] She had several intense relationships – with plenty of oomph – notably with television personalities Jonathan Routh and then with Alan Whicker to whom she was briefly engaged. The gossip columns implied that she had a liaison with Jennifer Patterson of culinary fame but probably that was just melodramatic press innuendo. Olga Deterding died in a London night-club on New Year's Eve, 1978.

৵৽৹

Schweitzer's capacity to appreciate people on their own terms is charmingly illustrated in the account of his friendship with Marion Preminger. He responded to her generosity of spirit towards him whilst nobody else could

---

[53] Sandra Jobson Darroch, *Ottoline: Life of Lady Ottoline Morrell* (Cassell, 1988), p.297.

bear the frivolous woman who wore make-up in the jungle.[54]

Schweitzer was not threatened by otherness. He did not need to attack it or change it into a replication of his own image which is our usual response to what does not suit us or does not confirm our own identity. That may account for his capacity to be charming to and be charmed by people who were completely unlike himself.

Schweitzer's delight in Marion Preminger makes an interesting contrast to, for instance, the atmosphere of the visit of Ruth Dayan, described below. Dayan felt immediate disdain towards Schweitzer, although she soon tempered her reaction, a reaction of which she supposed he was oblivious. Coincidentally, Dayan was in Lambaréné at the same time as Preminger. Dayan does not mention her.

Behind his back, Marion Preminger described Schweitzer as "a living saint". To his face, she treated him like a lover. Not very astonishingly, this worked a treat. Around them, everyone rolled their eyes.

Marion Preminger (1903-1972) was the glamorous, Hungarian, ex-wife of film mogul Otto Preminger whom she met in her youth in Vienna. They divorced in 1949 but throughout her later marriages, she held on to the conspicuous, door-opening surname of her first husband. She became addicted to drink, drugs, and affairs, attempting suicide three times before she moved back to Vienna to sort herself out. She met up with Schweitzer in Europe the year he was awarded the Nobel Peace Prize. He was in Paris to give his acceptance speech on being

---

[54] Louise Jilek-Aall, M.D., *Working with Dr Schweitzer* (Hancock House, 1990), ch. 6.

made a member of the prestigious French learned society, the Academy of Moral and Political Sciences.[55]

She "consulted" him weekly because she was going through a difficult period of her life. She subsequently became an active fund-raiser for the hospital, one of her first triumphs being to persuade American pharmaceutical companies to donate large amounts of stock.[56] According to the press, she annually visited "her hospital" in Lambaréné "to help with the lepers". The last seems hardly accurate if she is the same person entertainingly described by the level-headed Norwegian doctor, Louise Jilek-Aall. Jilek-Aall had been working with great courage as a "bush-nurse" in Tanganyika and war-torn Democratic Republic of Congo when she came to Lambaréné for six days' respite in in February 1961. Schweitzer warmed to her competence and intellect. She ended up staying for six months. She describes entertainingly how he annoyed everyone with his boyish excitement in Marion Preminger's *uber*-glossy company, scrubbing up and jaunting off to Lambaréné town *en pirogue* to spend time alone with her.

৽৽

Aside from the handful of professional reputation-trashers with their psychological problems, or with their

---

[55] *Académie des sciences morales et politiques.* The bestowal of the French honour after World War II contrasts with Schweitzer's status in 1923. At that time, because of his suspect pre-war German background, Victor Augagneur, Governor-General of AEF, declined Schweitzer's application for a visa to return to Lambaréné. Augagneur's term ended in August 1923 after which Schweitzer obtained his visa.

[56] Marion Preminger, *All I Want is Everything* (Funk & Wagnalls, 1957).

politically funded inducements, or with a compulsion to exhibit themselves as wittily superior to *le grand docteur*, there were also critics who had no outside agenda. The lasts' chatty injuries to Schweitzer's standing, and thus to both his funding and moral influence, were an accidental side-effect of their own self-regard.

An example of this is in, for instance, a book partly about Ruth Dayan. The author uses Dayan's input from notes she made fifty years before, applying a jaunty, irreverent tone in describing Schweitzer, a tone which may or may not be hers.[57]

In 1960 Ruth Dayan was still the wife of General Moshe Dayan (1915-1981). By the end of that year, she needed a break from her domestic environment.[58] Her husband's philandering was all over the tabloids and her young daughter had just published a supposedly salacious, barely disguised autobiographical novel. Dayan's concerned friend, Clara Urquhart, obtained for her an invitation to volunteer at the hospital. Some work to alleviate others' suffering, and some conversation with Schweitzer, might help Dayan salve the wounds.

What on earth was Clara Urquhart thinking? One could hardly conjure up two more ill-matched personalities to bring together. And so it proved.

As Dayan put it, they "took a rattletrap prop plane – 'a flying sardine can'" to Lambaréné. Schweitzer, with "a shock of white hair and a jackdaw perched on his shoulder", was waiting to greet them when their pirogues

---

[57] Anthony David, *An Improbable Friendship: the story of Yasser Arafat's mother-in-law,* [and] *the wife of Israel's top general, and their 40-year mission of peace* (Simon & Schuster, 2015), ch. 22.

[58] When they divorced in 1971, Moshe and Ruth Dayan had been estranged for years. He remarried in 1973.

first docked at the hospital landing.[59] Ruth Dayan is alternately haughtily amused or plain disgusted with what she encounters there. Her biographer writes:

> Among the first things she noticed about Schweitzer's compound was the rotting stench that pervaded everything, and the cultic behaviour of some of his followers. With the stultifying heat and afternoon downpours, the living, dying, decomposing vegetation, and the merciless struggle for existence – part of the compound was a leper colony – she realised that only the hardiest, and most idealistic of followers, or the looniest, could hack it. One doctor walked around with a monkey in his pocket, and a nurse shared her shack with a wildcat. Outside Ruth's hut, and next to the TB ward, sat a witch doctor casting evil spells against Schweitzer and his team for taking away his business. . . Ruth spent most of her time working in the orphanage with abandoned babies. (According to the local beliefs at the time, identical twins brought bad luck and were pitched into the forest.)[60]

Ruth Dayan admitted to her deliberate intention to resist Schweitzer's charisma, a quality of which she was wary. She was still unhappily married to a famously magnetic man. Although her attitude was later to soften, in the meantime her way of resisting the attraction was to make fun of Schweitzer. This would explain her likening

---

[59] The "jackdaw" must have been "Jackie" the magpie that Dr Goldwyn said "likes men" and took a fancy to alighting on his shoulder: "I frankly do not like it. . . He is everywhere." (12 November 1960.) When Emma Haussknecht was mortally ill, Jackie would knock on her door until someone opened it for him to visit her.

[60] David (2015), ch. 22. The last remark refers to a trauma in the life of a mother and her village. The birth of twins was regarded as a curse and one child "had" to die, usually the weaker. If one child got ill, the other was treated for the illness. Babies were "kept a long time until allegedly one of the two is poisoned" (Goldwyn, 11 November 1960).

the nightly dinner scene around the table to the tea party the mad-hatter gave in *Alice in Wonderland*, with Schweitzer in the role of the mad-hatter. While he went native in some things – his opposition to flush toilets for instance – when he sat down for a plate of crocodile fillets prepared in the German sauerbraten tradition, he spread a freshly laundered linen napkin on his lap, and carved the fillet on Alsatian china. Following the meal, everyone gathered in the room decorated with a cuckoo clock to sing Lutheran hymns. He played Bach toccatas on a warped, out-of-tune organ. . .[61]

The mockery is perhaps exaggerated by Dayan's biographer. Later, he has her admit that despite her finding Schweitzer odd, she thought that he was "immensely kind". She was touched by "the reigning pacifism of the hospital" and concluded that Schweitzer's integrity was the "opposite approach to life of Moshe's ego-driven will-to-power and worship of money". Above all, she liked that no one there, and especially not Schweitzer, "deferred to her as the wife of the general" – a declaration unfortunately open to interpretation.

Out of such incidental entertainments, misinformation spreads. For instance, Dayan censured Schweitzer's so-called "opposition to flush toilets" but that simply was inaccurate. It is always easier to presume an absence of thought in others than in oneself. The fact was, as explained by Brabazon, that pipes of running water

required a mechanical pump, and a pump meant fuel, spare parts, and a certain elementary understanding of and respect for machinery. Fuel was expensive – it had to be transported from Europe – and supplies were not guaranteed. . . and the flow could dry up, leaving the whole system useless. Spare parts were even less easily available. And every section of the system would be vulnerable to the ignorance and curiosity of tribesmen,

---

[61] David (2015), ch. 22.

who had never seen such a thing before and had no conception of its frailties. Better therefore an old fashioned well and a hand-pump one could rely on... [62]

Schweitzer's "opposition to flush toilets" was based on reason and experience. It had nothing to do with "going native", nor even, for that matter, to do with his moral preference for minimalism. He had grappled for decades to find the best answers to problems in the ever more populated hospital compound, problems and answers that a sceptical visitor would not have known were even there either because the practicalities of the context were beyond a stranger's ken or because the problems were moral ones that demanded an ethical solution. Schweitzer's reason for being there was only to alleviate suffering with the minimum of interference, without harming anything or anyone.

His visitor Ruth Dayan perpetuated the cartoonists' persona latterly projected on to him, the image of a comically gentle dreamer with perhaps a monkey on one shoulder and a bird on the other, a sort of betrousered Mother Teresa on safari.

To continue the comparison in all seriousness, his own mission was not nearly as grand as Anjezë Bojaxhiu's but ethically, it was far more ambitious. He was not omnipresent, as was "Mother Teresa". When she died in 1997, she'd put her name to missions in over a hundred countries. We should not forget the moral imperative that Schweitzer placed at the centre of his project. Whereas Mother Teresa flew around the world promoting her cause, literally extending her reach, Schweitzer declined to so much as step into an aeroplane, saw no point in motor-boats or the unnecessary use of cars. These views

---

[62] Brabazon (1976), pp. 341-342.

82

were consistent with his moral argument against doing harm.

Ethical change can only perpetuate itself when it swells up from a ground-force of people, not when it is imposed from on high. While Mother Teresa was a Catholic, following the tenets of her religion, he was a renegade Lutheran pastor, well-versed in philosophical and secular, socio-political texts. He did not regard the world as fully civilised. On the basis of his experience and his research, he concluded that civilisation – used as a transitive verb – requires action not words. We should do as we say. He was concerned not with replicating Eden. He was concerned with the urgent necessity of our applying our intellects to halt the inevitability of people suffering needlessly, or killing each other in war, or embarking on impersonal, global destruction.

ৎ৽৾

When Rhena Schweitzer took over the administration after his death, she had less experience of the place than many of the senior people working there. She shared her father's talent for practical solutions but did not prioritise the moral philosophy that underpinned his solutions. She could not have appreciated at the time that his decisions had evolved rationally over fifty years, were designed for that context, were always ethical, intelligent and functional. From the moment of his death there were several members of staff ready to continue doing things his way but the decision was out of their hands.

Rhena Schweitzer, having taken charge and having re-made the site, discovered that she could not remain there to keep it going for another fifty years. Her modernizing alterations ended his legacy there. It is a sad irony that while Schweitzer had spent so much of his precious time working to raise funds, after his death the funds – until they began to be channelled off course – were easier to depend upon than was the hospital's longevity.

Like her mother, Rhena Schweitzer moved house a great deal but while she retained her strong connections with Switzerland, America was the country that, with her second husband, she would make her own and it was where several of Schweitzer's grandchildren would grow up. Pacific Palisades could not be further from Lambaréné.

The "argument that was his life" hadn't had much influence on his biological family. Perhaps that is beside the point given that he had separated himself from them for most of his life. It is curious that, forceful and brilliant as he was, in the end he did not have the will to stipulate how his legacy should be upheld. In his last days, his staff waited nervously while he took a long time to get around to signing the document that gave his daughter administrative authority over his life's project.

The charitable organisations bearing his name continue to thrive faultlessly, fostering wide-ranging philanthropy. It would be tempting to regard the failed ending of the hospital as an indicator of his ideas' failure were it not that he had said explicitly that it wasn't necessary to come to Lambaréné to make a Lambaréné, that one could make a Lambaréné anywhere.

Perhaps at the end he predicted what would happen and was too worn out to care. Perhaps he heard his catch phrase differently at the end: "My life is my argument". Exactly. *His* "life". When it was over, it was over, as was all his fight.

ক০৵

Schweitzer had only ever wanted to shuck suspect, automatic, self-serving, materialistic preoccupations, to try to relieve people of physical suffering where possible, and to try not to harm living things. The awards, the accolades and the flummery had its flattering moments but, essentially, they were the reasons that the hospital had an income. He would have been the first to see the irony of this and the terrible trap it set. The hospital's survival was predicated upon what certain white people needed to imagine about him. He always struggled to control his own distaste for actions that did not respect the difference of others. That comfortable world of money was the very one he had sought to escape and it was the one that concocted heroic or villainous versions of him. If he wanted funding from those quarters, and he was in no position to be choosy, he had to learn to navigate its polluted waters.

A handy example which took place in the period to which we keep coming back, is the visit of Adlai Stevenson (1900-1965). Schweitzer's inescapable compromises are embedded in this relatively small scene, again replete with soap opera potential, in which it only requires a little imagination to guess at the discomfort that Schweitzer had to put aside.

Stevenson (to whom we will return more seriously in the next section) arrived in Lambaréné at the end of his African tour, on 21 June 1957. He had a plane-load of travelling companions. These were his daughter-in-law Nancy Stevenson, his lover Marietta Tree, her husband Sir Ronald Tree, Marietta's sixteen-year-old daughter, Frances FitzGerald, Stevenson's law partner William McCormick Blair, his wife, Deeda, Maurice Tempelsman – a diamond expert, and last but not least, Alicia Patterson

(1906-1963), the founder in 1940 of *Newsday*.[63] Alicia and Adlai Stevenson had been involved romantically, intermittently, since she was nineteen and he was twenty-five. (Stevenson's wife had died in 1949.) In 1939, Alicia Patterson had married Harry Frank Guggenheim, both of them marrying for the third time. (Coincidentally, as we noticed earlier, after divorcing Frank Catchpool, Adriana married the widower of Nancy, Harry Frank Guggenheim's daughter by his first marriage.)

Stevenson's group had chartered a DC-4 from Lisbon, flying first to Johannesburg where they were hosted by Sir Harry Oppenheimer. After visiting Kimberley, they flew to Salisbury where they were hosted by Sir Ian Smith (who became Prime Minister of Rhodesia in 1964), flew to Zanzibar, were hosted by colonial officials in Tanganyika, Uganda, Kenya and the Belgian Congo's Leopoldville (Kinshasa). Next, in Brazzaville, the French Governor-General Léo Pétillon laid on "the finest banquet of the trip, two hundred guests, mostly European, barrels of Bélon oysters, fresh *asperges,* and a dance band this time flown in from Paris".[64] (In Nairobi, a band had been flown in from Cairo.) Alicia Patterson found the extravagance distasteful.

Lambaréné was to be the highlight of the tour. In her party's earlier forays into self-congratulatory colonial enclaves, she was derisively amused by the vulgar displays of opulence. At Lambaréné, she was scandalised, for the opposite reason. The place was insanitary. What's more, Schweitzer greeted them wearing "a grimy doctor's smock". (No Bélon oysters and dance band there, then.)

---

[63] See A. Arlen and M. Arlen, *The Huntress: The Adventures, Escapades, and Triumphs of Alicia Patterson* (Pantheon, 2016), pp. 287ff.
[64] Patterson quotations, *ibid.*

She found his manner with patients almost disdainful. She was particularly irritated that Adlai Stevenson's awe of Schweitzer remained intact.

We need never suppose that Schweitzer was unaware of how he was perceived. Alicia Patterson supposed her response was undetectable.

She remained oblivious of the fact that she was an integral part of what she derided, a cog in a system with its contradictions but all of a political piece. She herself was a privileged tourist looking on from on high, from the distance of a privately chartered plane, if you like, and all that it implied.

Schweitzer was never a finger-pointing dirt-kicker. He would never have singled out Alicia Patterson for a disdainful *ad hominem* attack. But then, the broad disposition of chess pieces presented a difficulty. It was upon such people, often, that his hospital funding depended and in this instance, upon such people that the dissemination of his ethical protest against nuclear testing depended. Such people may have been rich, privileged, and unwittingly self-righteous – but they were ultimately well-meaning. He had to find a moral approach route – without stepping on too many insects.

An ethical path was elusive. Perhaps he had always to live with the sense of failure induced by the contradiction. He needed such people. Perhaps he offered his hospitality, wearing his grubby smock, in the same spirit that he had let the thief back into the compound. I surmise. He would never have said so out loud. But he probably served them crocodile for lunch.

7

Anti-Nuclear Protest

LET us keep foremost in our minds that this eccentric genius had once meant to get himself away to the ends of the earth, to focus on quietly doing a little, with difficulty, but well. Eventually he found his ethical practice entangled in a not very distant political and economic struggle.

Schweitzer had always avoided taking sides in political matters because, he held, usually political power was wielded by those who owned it, against the people, instead of the other way around.

In January 1954 and again in November that year in his Nobel Peace Prize acceptance speech (he went to Oslo to collect it only two years after the award), to everyone's surprise, he entered the margins of the political arena. He expressed his concern about nuclear weapons. He had been doing research into the effect of radiation fallout from nuclear test explosions on the atmosphere, soil and sea. The resulting calculations were alarming, predicting an ongoing and worsening catastrophe.

In February 1957, Clara Urquhart brought American publisher Norman Cousins to Lambaréné.[65] They were both active in the early phase of the international movement for nuclear disarmament. He had been a consultant to Democratic presidential candidate

---

[65] Norman Cousins (1960), pp. 171ff.

Adlai Stevenson and was later to advise President Kennedy on the subject of nuclear testing.

Urquhart was as well aware as anyone who knew Schweitzer that he never took the easy way out of a big problem by sticking to a preconception but would think through anew the ethical implications of each case. As far as she could predict, there was as much of a chance that he would change his mind as not when it came to publicly supporting the growing anti-nuclear lobby. Cousins and Urquhart intended to persuade him out of his political reticence, to add his name to the list of prominent signatories to the protest. His moral standing would add great weight to it.

At first, they saw no sign that Schweitzer would accede to their request. A few days later, he initiated a new discussion with them. If he were to support the protest, it should not be merely another generalised objection to nuclear arms, as they had put it to him, but should have a clearly defined, realisable target. What he had in mind was an objection to nuclear testing in particular, an objection put forward in April 1956 by Adlai Stevenson, with whom Schweitzer had been corresponding. Nuclear tests generated catastrophic effects of radiation fallout upon the earth, the seas and in the atmosphere. Of course, without testing there would be no nuclear advances.

Schweitzer wanted the method by which his opinion would be disseminated to make optimal impact with minimal display. Lavish conferences, majestic interviews, grand statements where big cheeses mouthed worthy words, were anathema to him. Change had to come from the grassroots, from the people themselves protesting that nuclear fallout violated international law and caused harm. After some thought he decided that the best means to convey his opinion appropriately was for his words to be read on a broadcast from a small radio station that could be picked up and used afterwards by different communication systems.

On both counts, the message and the medium, Cousins and Urquhart took his point.

Henceforth, the radiation effects of nuclear testing became the primary angle of attack of what was to become the world-wide Campaign for Nuclear Disarmament (CND). Schweitzer's name was associated thereafter with the movement and its sister organisations.

Schweitzer's friend, Albert Einstein, died on 18 April 1957, soon after the meeting in Lambaréné with Cousins and Urquhart. Einstein's death was a great loss to the embryonic movement's aim to use international luminaries of the highest rank to bolster anti-nuclear protest. Fortunately, there remained many others, amongst them Bertrand Russell and Canon Collins in Britain and Linus Pauling in America.[66] Because Schweitzer is no longer the household name he was then, today we cannot appreciate the full political impact of his agreeing to support the movement for nuclear disarmament.

On 23 April 1957, Radio Oslo broadcast his "Declaration of Conscience", Schweitzer's first widely publicised speech, from the city that awarded the Nobel Peace Prize.[67] He focussed on the hazards of nuclear

---

[66] Linus Pauling won the Nobel Prize for Chemistry in 1954 and was to win it again for Peace in 1962 for his work opposing nuclear testing. He and his wife, Ava Helen, visited Lambaréné in 1959.

[67] In May1958 he wrote three more Oslo radio talks, entitled "The Renunciation of Nuclear Tests", "The Danger of an Atomic War" and "Negotiations at the Highest Level". With his 1957 "Declaration of Conscience", they were subsequently

radiation to everyone in the world. The speech was translated, published and re-broadcast in some fifty countries – but not in America. There the dangers he warned of were trivialised and the speech was reprinted merely in a few liberal newspapers.

Polls uncovered that a preponderance of ordinary Americans favoured a test-ban treaty with Moscow. The average person was worried about the dangers of nuclear testing.[68] In January 1958 Linus Pauling presented a protest petition to the UN Secretary-General, Dag Hammarskjöld. It had been signed by thirty-six Nobel laureates and over nine thousand scientists around the world.

Schweitzer's talks caused agitation in the US State Department. Nuclear arms superiority was a lynchpin of Eisenhower's administration. They saw the lobby to stop nuclear testing as being the latest Communist line to seduce the masses. State Department documents declassified in the 1990s reveal that Schweitzer's stand was profoundly disagreeable to the government. His letters were intercepted. The Albert Schweitzer Fellowship fundraising organisation was investigated – but it was found only to be what it said on the tin. When the acting US Consul-General to the Congo logged in May 1958 that he was going to visit Schweitzer, he was told to "exercise extreme caution" and on no account to discuss nuclear matters. He ignored the instruction and delivered a reassuring report about the visit. A year later Eisenhower had reversed his position on nuclear testing,

published – in America, when it changed its tune for a short while – as a book entitled *Peace or Atomic War?*
[68] Benjamin P. Greene, *Eisenhower, Science Advice, and the Nuclear Test-ban Debate, 1945-1963*, p.123.

ostensibly.[69] Within a few years, the CND and its sister movements had a massive international following.

❧

Within six months of Norman Cousins meeting Schweitzer, the initial shape of the protest movement had become defined. At a meeting in New York on 21 June 1957, Cousins and Clarence Pickett formally established the National Committee for a Sane Nuclear Policy (SANE). There was an apparent resurgence of McCarthyism, with SANE's members being suspected of being Communists when really, the objective was the promotion of a "mutuality of interest in survival" beyond any "ideological or power rivalries".[70]

Around the same time, a month after the Oslo broadcast of Schweitzer's "Declaration of Conscience" (and a couple of weeks after my father had left Lambaréné), Adlai Stevenson, the American Democratic presidential candidate who had recently lost to Eisenhower, arrived there with his friends.

Stevenson had met Schweitzer in Chicago in July 1949 at a grand luncheon at which seventeen hundred people had paid to listen to a speech given by the "Man of God". On 21 June 1957, Stevenson and his entourage arrived on their chartered plane. It was the end of his African tour and he had three days in which to talk alone with Schweitzer, by whom he was enthralled. This made a change since it was usually Stevenson who was enthralling everyone in his orbit.

[69] Lawrence S. Wittner, "Blacklisting Schweitzer", *Bulletin of Atomic Scientists* (May-June 1995), pp. 55-60.
[70] Dario Fazzi, *Eleanor Roosevelt and the Anti-Nuclear Movement* (Macmillan, 2016), p.158.

The two men had common concerns. Stevenson, who had consulted closely with Norman Cousins, had publicly proposed in April 1956 that America cease nuclear testing and persuade other prospective nuclear powers to do the same. Eisenhower had silenced him with the contemptuous assertion that America had to ensure by every means its military superiority in a threatening world. Six months later Stevenson was running for president on the promise that if he were elected, his first deed would be to promulgate a nuclear test ban. Eisenhower won the election and was inaugurated in January 1957. He had it both ways in terms of the increasingly nervous electorate: the following year, Eisenhower and the Russians agreed on a nuclear moratorium with the aim of agreeing on a test ban treaty. In 1963, the Kennedy administration, advised by Stevenson and Cousins, ratified the Partial Test Ban Treaty. In due course, nuclear deterrence took precedence over test bans as the basis of America's security policy.

Schweitzer always said that one had to lead by example, not with talk. While he had in small or large ways influenced thousands of people with the example of how he tried to live with "reverence for life", by 1965, despite its grass-roots expansion, the anti-nuclear lobby had hardly altered the actions of the powerful. Rhena Schweitzer said that when her father was dying, he said his greatest sorrow was that all his effort had done nothing to stop the development of nuclear arms.[71]

There has since been much complicated to-ing and fro-ing on the matter across the world. The outcome, in brief, is that the Comprehensive Test Ban Treaty of 1996, given the paucity of signatures, is unenforceable.

---

[71] Rhena Schweitzer Miller (1986), p.25.

8

White Man in Africa

THE instability of Schweitzer's reputation in his last years owed much to a cause that is more disturbing than, say, accusations of his being an eccentric German missionary running an unhygienic hospital for black people to whom he was rude.

The immediate post-independence conflict in central Africa amounted to nothing less than a proxy war between the two strongest military powers in the world at the time, the Western alliance and Moscow. For the men in real power (those with real power were all male), it was convenient to have Schweitzer's image sullied. There were unanswered questions about how close he was to the politics of the Democratic Republic of Congo (DRC). How much did he know about what was secretly going on there? Was he in bed with the Russians?

Whatever Schweitzer knew, he was a threat only in moral terms but in a jumpy organisation, by definition, where there's smoke there must be fire. The account below will confirm that the West's strategy for fending off possible danger was simply to eliminate the putative problem whether it took the form of an eccentric white jungle doctor or, as we shall see, the genuine, democratically elected leader of an African country.

It was plain to everyone that post-independence Africa was hardly a happy counterweight to the despair of anti-nuclear lobbyists. The new perpetrators may have had unfamiliar faces but independent Africa was full of the same horrors as historical, colonial Africa. In February 1964 in Gabon, an attempted coup against the dictatorial conduct of the fairly new President Léon M'ba, beloved of de Gaulle, was led by left-leaning Jean-Hilaire Aubame. M'ba and Aubame were both Fang, and had known each other since childhood.

The sympathetic military, in support of Aubame, brought M'ba to Lambaréné town. (He was meant to be taken to Ndjole but torrential rain prevented that.) There the government heralded Aubame as the country's new leader. Aubame notified the French ambassador, Paul Cousseran, that foreign nationals and their property would be protected and French military intervention must be avoided. But M'ba was a creature of the French. De Gaulle intervened with the help of the infamous Jacques Foccart (of the "Machiavellian hand", according to his *New York Times* obituary). M'ba was re-instated. Aubame was imprisoned and beaten up.

This is all by way of some contrasting background to what a man like Schweitzer stood for in the region. The political pattern repeated in Gabon what had been enacted not long before on a larger and more brutal scale in the nearby Democratic Republic of Congo. It will be discussed in the next section because it bears on the means by which Schweitzer's name was shifted out of the limelight and into a dusty corner of the hall of fame.

భావ

No doubt Schweitzer's life's project failed in many respects but the failure was not very much in the places where fingers have been pointed. During most of his life-time, relatively little value was accorded his philosophical writings, which in his view were amongst the most worthwhile of his achievements. He was immensely well-read. On the basis of his studies and his experience, he concluded that our universal ethical obligation is to avoid cultural and ecological destruction of any living thing on land or sea or air. His *raison d'être,* his entire life, had been shaped by these beliefs. They were the reason that he had laboured to originate the hospital. He supposed that by being a living example of these beliefs, others would be encouraged to recognise their soundness and do as he did. Yet even of those who lived close to him, a mere handful shared his quotidian integrity. How difficult we find it to do good, not just now and then but every day.

What did he think, one must wonder, when at the end of his life, he looked upon all that mankind had made, and behold, it was very bad. It was worse, not better, than when he had first embarked for Africa. How ironic that he was right there in 1960 when, ostensibly, the country of Gabon was given the opportunity to start anew, under its own auspices, with a clean slate. Like so many others, the new government did not fully appreciate its own indigenous variety of cultures, values and traditions. Almost continuously since its independence and to this day, Gabon's government has remained in the hands of the same family.

In newly independent countries at that time, many of the leaders continued as if whites knew best – that is to say, those leaders who were not removed by political sleight of hand or even simply assassinated for resisting neo-colonisation. Those who seized so-called power all too often were either bought by foreigners or else fell hook, line and sinker for the propaganda of foreigners.

The new leaders did not allow themselves time – or were not allowed it – to protect themselves from alien incursions. There was seldom a sign of deliberation upon the kind of appropriate, genuinely independent society they might fruitfully originate out of the hard lessons learned from an exploited past. Worse still, as we shall see in the example below of the DRC, when the United Nations was called on to help the country gain time to consolidate peacefully, the UN failed to respond sympathetically and the result was, and remains, catastrophic.

One does not talk lightly of exploitation, political failure, and assassination. When Schweitzer used his exceptional mind to propose a way to halt the advance of horror, he was not embarking on a flight of fancy to serve the founding of an agrarian idyll. He held that the usual notion of ameliorating post-independence poverty by pumping foreign money into an infrastructure that served only foreign investment, was of no avail to ordinary people. What was required was a thorough-going move to alter our fundamental attitudes, to eradicate the selfish premises by which we live, and above all to let people make their own choices within their small communities.

Today, everything that Schweitzer introduced at his Lambaréné hospital has gone. Practical medical help, a politically neutral refuge for belligerent ethnic groups, a community trying to practice reverence for life – none of this has survived him there.

The explanation is manifold. It includes the sad inability of generous philanthropy to alter society for the good in the long-term. It includes local politicians' unexamined emulation of neo-colonial values, imitation that leads, incrementally, to massive corruption, and worse. Meanwhile, the beneficiaries of those criminal acts pretend that their acts either didn't happen or were a necessary means to a supposedly productive end.

Schweitzer had become accustomed – but not inured – to depending financially on well-meaning people most of whose values he did not share. That compromise was as nothing compared to the political manoeuvres he was witnessing at work in the region, destructive powers that, he at last had to concede, would not even be a little dented by his one-man-show of "reverence for life".

The *dénouement* was surely uncannily familiar to him. As a young theological student, he had written about a man long ago who had tried to do good and given his life to that cause, believing that it would produce a ripple effect of morality in his community. In the end the good man found himself betrayed and forsaken. At the time of his dying, he had to submit to the agony of knowing that his life's work had not brought salvation to anyone at all. If his life had had any value, it was merely the effect he had had fleetingly on others in his day to day life.

During his last years, Schweitzer's cynicism about the consequences of so-called political independence confirmed his suspicion about the ruinous manipulations of the Western allies in Africa generally, and in nearby Democratic Republic of Congo in particular. To know something about what was going on there, is to understand the rest more fully.

9

The CIA, Belgium, and the Congo

EISENHOWER and even Kennedy's CIA and the U.S. State Department suspected that Schweitzer had Communist sympathies – which he certainly did not. Nevertheless, to them, he was *persona non grata*. This was a period when the nuclear arms race was at the centre of American foreign policy, given America's anxiety about remaining the superior power in the Cold War.

Over his life-time, Schweitzer had been seen as an exceptional moral example to the world. Since 1947, with the American press leading the way, he had been described as a humanitarian, a saint, "the greatest man in the world".

By February 1958, when the British CND was launched, the movement was already an instrument to be reckoned with. If Schweitzer's image were damaged, it would help erode his contribution to the current popularization of the anti-nuclear lobby. Best of all would be just to remove him from the picture. He was a nicely conspicuous target, easy to hit because of his apparent eccentricity and conveniently remote from instant metropolitan support. As we noted earlier, the U.S. State Department took to opening his mail and investigated the Albert Schweitzer Fellowship. A couple of publications by right-wing journalists about an odd old man who had gone native in the wilds provided marketable, nastily amusing, iconoclastic stories repeated in the international press just as had been the earlier stories of his sanctity.

To those who worried about such things, Schweitzer's objection to Western political interference in the Democratic Republic of Congo[72] must have seemed all of a piece with his objection to nuclear arms testing.

How to catch out Schweitzer? Slowly and consistently.

In 1961, he wrote a courtesy letter to Walter Ulbricht, the Stalinist-style head of state in East Germany. He was acknowledging Ulbricht's good wishes regarding the honorary degree that the prestigious Humboldt University had conferred on Schweitzer. The university had a chequered past, having been hijacked first by the Nazis and then by the Soviets during the Cold War. Ulbricht, seizing the chance for some self-promotion, published the letter, manipulating an instance of Schweitzer's good manners and ever-conscientious letter-writing to give the impression that Schweitzer was a Communist sympathiser. It didn't help that Schweitzer had recently been in correspondence with Adlai Stevenson about the inadvisability of America making Russia anxious by surrounding East Germany with nuclear missiles.

Then in 1962, contrary to his usual mode, and signalling his strength of feeling about the matter, Schweitzer deliberately put himself in a political spotlight. He sent a letter to the liberal newspaper in Belgium, *La Dernière Heure*, describing his objections to overseas

---

[72] The DRC was formerly the Belgian Congo and is not to be confused with the Republic of the Congo which lies between Gabon and DRC. The Republic of the Congo, formerly part of French Equatorial Africa, is sometimes called Congo Brazzaville. Confusion arises because since pre-colonial times the lay term for the whole undifferentiated region has remained "the Congo".

governments interfering with the politics of Gabon's near neighbour, the DRC.

To make sense of the gravity of the views Schweitzer wanted to express in his letter, one needs to take a detour into the politics of post-colonial Africa into events that so distressed him that he saw fit to break his pledge with himself to avoid the mire of political statements. What follows is an attempt to summarise a fragment of an unsettling history whose most awful aspects have been uncovered only recently.

When the Democratic Republic of Congo gained political independence from Belgium in June 1960, Patrice Lumumba (1925-1961), a socialist who favoured a centralised government, was elected as the DRC's prime minister.[73] Joseph Kasavubu (1917-1969), a capitalist who favoured a federal form of government, was elected president to stand alongside him. At the time, the DRC was divided into four antagonistic provinces. Moise Tshombe was leader of Katanga province in the south, the region richest in gold, diamonds, copper, cobalt and other minerals, where most foreign investment was located. The Belgian company Union Minière had long held a 7,700 square mile mining concession in Katanga that included a mine at Shinkolobwe, to which we shall return.

About a week after the DRC became independent, Tshombe declared the secession of Katanga from the rest

---

[73] The novelist Barbara Kingsolver lived in the Belgian Congo as a child. *The Poisonwood Bible* (1998) evokes the region's changing political atmosphere from a small girl's viewpoint. She constructs a romanticised but heartfelt portrait of a character representing a young Lumumba.

of the country. Lumumba supported national unity. He could see trouble ahead, what with internal factional fighting spreading and pressure from Western interests exacerbating divisions. He called on the United Nations to bring in troops to stabilise the situation.

After long deliberation, the Secretary-General of the United Nations, Dag Hammarskjöld, upheld the UN's brief to remain neutral regarding a country's internal politics. He refused to send troops to help Lumumba.

It might be said that this was in character: Hammarskjöld had not covered himself in glory during the Hungarian crisis of 1 November 1956 when Imre Nagy asked the United Nations for support in the face of the threat of invading Soviet tanks. Nagy's request was only looked at after the Soviets had invaded and anyway it was rejected. Eighteen months later, he was executed by the Communists.

Lumumba seemed likely to turn to Moscow for support instead, which was anathema to the Belgian mining companies in Katanga. They neither wanted their assets nationalised by Lumumba, nor did they want to see the Soviets move in. The Belgians ordered Kasavubu to sack Lumumba. The parliament voted for him to stay. In the midst of this disarray, pawn of the Western allies, army commander Sese Seko Mobutu (as he later named himself) stepped in and arrested Lumumba. UN troops watched as he was physically beaten. Then he was murdered.

Very much later an investigative writer produced evidence that the Belgian Minister of African Affairs, Count d'Aspremont, had ordered Lumumba to be sent to Katanga where on 17 January 1961 Belgian officers executed him, watched by Tshombe. The deed was not done by Tshombe's men, as was reported at the time.[74]

With Lumumba's murder, support for his movement grew and faction fighting continued across the country. Now Hammarskjöld began working with the DRC central government to end the attempted secession of Katanga, this time promising the help of United Nations troops so that the central government could retain possession of the wealth of the whole country.

Hammarskjöld's UN cohort was the Dubliner Conor Cruise O'Brien, a gifted, bibulous diplomat and writer, who joked about the gin and the hunting. He blundered in, a white man without a clue about Africa. Under his watch, there were two main UN military assaults against the secessionists. The first was on 28 August 1961, code-named Operation Rumpunch, a small success for the central government.

A cable of 10 September 1961 shows that in sending in UN troops to help the central government, Hammarskjöld was breaching the UN's legal mandate. He was loath to admit it, supposedly, when he was brought to book by both President Kennedy and Prime Minister Macmillan.

Three days later, on 13 September 1961, UN troops and central government forces conducted a second assault, called Operation Morthor. It was a disaster.[75]

On 18 September 1961, Hammarskjöld was killed in a "pilot error" plane crash over Northern Rhodesia (later

---

[74] See Ludo de Witte, *The Assassination of Lumumba* (1999; Verso, 2001). The book prompted the Belgian government's Lumumba Commission of Enquiry into whether Belgium was involved in his murder.
[75] Michael Kennedy and Art Magennis, *Ireland, the United Nations and the Congo: a military and diplomatic history, 1960–1961* (Four Courts, 2014).

Zambia). Eye witnesses reported, although it has never been confirmed officially, that the small plane was shot down by white men in combat uniform. In 2011, a Swedish aid worker, Göran Björkdahl, produced documentary evidence that Hammarskjöld had been murdered for the benefit of the mining companies.

At the end of 1961, Conor Cruise O'Brien resigned from his UN posting. In 1964 in the *New York Review of Books,* he took the trouble to review a peculiar book by Gerald McKnight that trashed everything about Schweitzer. Even O'Brien, who himself persisted in a strange antagonism towards Schweitzer, thought that McKnight's book spoke more of the author's suspect obsessionalism than of the subject himself which makes it tempting to believe the conspiracy theory that McKnight was paid to write a book that blemished Schweitzer's name.

O'Brien persisted in his own equally benighted – forgive the pun – hand-me-down, under-researched, drubbing of Schweitzer.[76] Much is explained by the fact that it was only three years since O'Brien had made his literally murderous hatchet job as the United Kingdom's UN representative in Katanga. It must have rankled O'Brien that Schweitzer had from the start, been right. Schweitzer well understood the terrible complexity of the situation that Hammarskjöld and the UN were expected to resolve. He had written to Hammarskjöld telling him that it was misguided to force the unification of Katanga with the rest of the Congo. That his views coincided with Belgium's was for Belgium merely a happy accident: their motives could not have been more unlike.

---

[76] In the late 1960s O'Brien was not above accepting the post of Albert Schweitzer Professor of Humanities at New York University.

Schweitzer stood his ground regarding his support of Tshombe's bid to secede even when his illustrious, liberal comrades, including Bertrand Russell, his much-respected anti-nuclear colleague, were telling him he was ill-informed and wrong. They claimed, from their distant eyries, that the correct political, economic, and humanitarian strategy was to force unification of the country. Schweitzer knew well that the country was nothing of the sort, that its boundaries had not been made by the people who lived there but by ruthless imperialist invaders in their scramble for Africa.[77]

His friends changed their minds later, when it was too late. Schweitzer was proved right, again. His predictions were the product of information and logic, not prophecy.

In February 1963, just after UN troops and government soldiers had vanquished the would-be secessionist Tshombe, Schweitzer was still arguing with Bertrand Russell that Tshombe and Katanga should be left to their own devices. That year Tshombe fled the DRC, made a comeback as prime minister in 1964-1965 and soon fled again. Mobutu sentenced him to death *in absentia*. Tshombe died in puzzling circumstances in Algeria in June 1969.

---

[77] In 1885, the monstrous King Leopold II of Belgium acquired as his own private fiefdom a region that he called his Congo Free State. In the pursuit of wealth, mainly then in rubber plantations, atrocities against the workers were conducted with his knowledge. It was hearing of this from Hélène Bresslau at the start of the century that had alerted Schweitzer to the debt Europeans owed to central Africa. In 1908, the Belgian government annexed the territory from the King.

Back in 1965, Mobutu staged a coup against Kasavubu and proclaimed himself head of state. For the next thirty-two years, Mobutu was paid off by America and Belgium in return for their access to Katanga's mineral wealth.

Perhaps being intelligent, powerful, and having to live under the thumb of brutal foreigners, induces a brutal form of madness. Whatever the cause, Mobuto became a grotesque fabulist, drunk on spending the state's wealth as if it were his own. He squandered three or six or eight billion dollars (as variously cited) on his Cecil B. DeMille imperial fantasies at home and abroad. He was a sort of murderous version of King Ludwig II of Bavaria, with much worse taste.[78] Meanwhile the people were destitute and dying. It is the same today, except that now the mines dig deeper.

The mining profits of the country were so great that even while Mobutu milked it for a fortune, it continued as a financial honey-pot for Western companies. The DRC, or Zaire, as Mobutu re-named it between 1971 and 1997, served also as a strategically situated US military base from which to wage war against Soviet-backed African governments. Proxy American-Russian wars as well as internecine wars raged in and around the country while in Shinkolobwe in Katanga, the mines operated day and night to empty them speedily. By 1966, global politics and nuclear science had shifted. Shinkolobwe's ore, although valuable, as will be explained below, was no longer as urgently needed by the West as it had been. Mobutu no longer had to be courted.

---

[78] Mobutu's first wife, whom he married when she was fourteen, was of his ethnic group. As the country was then a French colony, she had been given a French name. After independence, she refused to take an African name, despite Mobutu's insistence. Her name was Marie-Antoinette.

In 1997 Mobutu was ousted by Laurent Kabila, who allegedly had been earning a living by engaging in gold smuggling and running a brothel in Tanzania.

Many years earlier, on 24 April 1965 to be precise, it had been the young rebel Laurent Kabila with whom Che Guevara and a hundred of his Cuban soldiers had joined forces in their legendary military escapade in Africa. Guevara hoped to help replicate the quick success of the Cuban revolution. Guevara found that Kabila, as he put it, "lacked revolutionary seriousness". Nor could he be relied upon to lead his men into completing pre-planned military attacks. The DRC's Marxist rebellion did not succeed. After seven months' fighting, Che and his men departed. Factional wars escalated.

Laurent Kabila's dictatorship was short-lived but that was to make no difference to the people of the country. He was assassinated by his guards in 2001 and his son Joseph Kabila took his place so effectively that any number of commentators on the region are unaware that they are not one and the same man.

As I write this, Joseph Kabila is still president of the DRC. He refused to relinquish power at the end of his term in 2016. Elections are scheduled for the end of 2017 but nobody's holding his breath. The government is repressive and the country is still at war with itself, the conflicts supposedly boosted by neighbouring Rwanda and Uganda. The numerous government and unidentified armed groups terrorizing civilians are rated internationally as the worst perpetrators of human rights violations. To date the largest UN Peacekeeping Mission in the world, numbering 19,000 soldiers, is stationed in the DRC.[79]

---

[79] Human Rights Watch keeps a record of DRC atrocities.

In 1999, it was historian Ludo de Witte who published documentary evidence that it was not Tshombe's men who had killed Lumumba as had hitherto been said, but Belgian agents. De Witte discovered that in August 1960, separately, President Eisenhower instructed the CIA chief, Allen Dulles, to have Lumumba murdered.[80] In September 1960, the British Foreign Office, separately, recorded that Lumumba's murder could solve the Katanga problem. De Witte found proof that, separately again, the murder plot [81]was hatched finally by the Belgian government's Count d'Aspremont. The plan was funded by the mining company, Union Minière, by then owned jointly by Belgian, American and British investors. Union Minière had transferred $35 million, originally meant for Lumumba's government, into Tshombe's personal bank account. In 2002 Belgium apologised for its role in the atrocity. In 2014, the CIA acknowledged its part in it. The subtext to the atrocities was always the proxy war between Washington and Moscow.

༺༻

If America's interest in the Democratic Republic of Congo still seems inexplicably excessive, and if you are wondering what all this has to do with Schweitzer and the CIA's suspicion of him, all is explained thus: it was not merely Katanga's gold, diamonds, copper or cobalt and

---

[80] CIA chief Allen Dulles' brother, John Foster Dulles, was Secretary of State in Eisenhower's government during this period.
[81] Six years after the murder, Harold d'Aspremont Lynden was dead at the young age of 53; his wife, age 51, died two months later.

"other minerals" that they were after, as valuable as those were.

It had recently been discovered that the mine at Shinkolobwe yielded a unique uranium ore.

That it yielded radium had been known as far back as 1911. Uranium had been mined there since 1915 for use in cancer treatments. Up to 1928, Belgium controlled the world's supply of uranium. In 1940, the Nazis marched into Belgium and gained control of its uranium refinery. Union Minière moved its headquarters to New York.

During World War II, mining operations in Katanga intensified because scientists in America had recently discovered that Shinkolobwe's uranium was of a purity that surpassed that of any other uranium mine in the world. It was exactly what they needed for making nuclear weapons as speedily as possible. The bombs dropped on Hiroshima and Nagasaki were made using uranium from Shinkolobwe.

During World War II, the Americans deemed it urgent to develop the so-called atom bomb swiftly lest the Nazis overtake them. After the War, they felt the same anxiety about the Soviets overtaking them.

By the late 1960s, the interest in Shinkolobwe had diminished because nuclear weaponry ceased to rely on the unique quality of the uranium mined there.[82] By the 1970s the mineshafts had been plugged with concrete and the area was guarded - or not, as writer Tom Zoellner found out in 2007 when he went there himself. Zoellner ascertained that decades before, miners had re-opened some shafts and had been routinely smuggling their radio-

---

[82] Aside from uranium and other minerals, during WWII, the former Belgian Congo provided rubber for the Allies as well as $28.5 million from its gold mines.

active booty across the border, mainly through Zambia, to sell on the black market, to who knows who.[83]

Back when Shinkolobwe was a closely guarded secret, how much did Schweitzer know about what was happening in his back yard? Even now, with the benefit of hindsight and progressively declassified information, it is difficult to get the story straight. Partly this is because its content depends on the loyalties of the story-teller and the story has so many sides, with most of its characters having tracks to cover.

Schweitzer could have maintained his familiar silence. Instead he very deliberately made a public statement in support of Tshombe and the secession of Katanga when he sent that letter to *La Dernière Heure.* He obviously had no inclination to support Union Minière in its continued fiefdom. On the eve of United Nations troops being sent into the Congo, his article was published in translation in the *Chicago Tribune.* Accompanied by an unusually grim, un-twinkly mug-shot of him, it appeared alongside other articles about the Congo and UN troops going into battle against Tshombe.[84]

Schweitzer's position reads as his usual wise counsel in a wicked world: leave well alone, let the people decide for themselves, don't force federalism if the people want to be separate. The designated borders were based on old European, imperial relations that had nothing to do with the two hundred and fifty different ethnic groups

[83] Tom Zoellner, *Uranium: War, Energy, and the Rock that Shaped the World* (Penguin, 2009); and Susan Williams, *Spies in the Congo: the race for the ore that built the atomic bomb* (Hurst, 2016).

[84] *Chicago Tribune* (20 December 1962), pp. 1-2. Disquieting to our current sensibilities is the ease with which leaders of the powerful nations openly debated how best they should configure the political affairs of another country, the DRC.

inhabiting the land, speaking their seven hundred languages.

The high-grade uranium mine at the time was top secret. Schweitzer, for all his well-connected connections, perhaps did *not* know the classified information about its unique importance in the production of nuclear weapons. Whether or not he knew, given his commitment to halting nuclear testing, we can't ignore the irony that the material source of the catastrophe he warned of was almost on his doorstep. The CIA did not see any irony. They saw an odd coincidence and found it suspect. It was one thing to argue for the secession of Katanga and it was quite another to suggest that Western investors simply get out of Katanga completely: that would open the way for the Soviets to fill the vacuum. This was certainly not what Union Minière had in mind when they backed Tshombe's bid for Katanga's secession.

If Schweitzer did know the secret, he would have supposed that the Russians were no more of a threat than was the West. One invading force was much like another. He probably had no idea that Tshombe would be bribed with $35 million to accede to the wishes of the foreigners.

Imagine if Schweitzer's words, by some magic, had had immediate effect and all the foreigners had left the DRC. Imagine that Tshombe and the rest of the country had been left to sort things out themselves, without foreign bribes and foreign troops. Imagine if the DRC, or any one of its African neighbours, had been left to find its own way, for its own good, as any Western country supposes it is entitled to do. Imagine if everyone tried to have reverence for life.

Schweitzer's phrase was shorthand for the proposition that our reason should orientate our conduct towards trying not to harm anyone or kill anything. That includes the idea that good fences make good neighbours. He was a proponent of anti-globalisation *avant la lettre.* He understood the benefits of the respectful acknowledgement of difference, of small worlds, clear boundaries, each individual's moral practice rather than the imposition of authoritarian rule.

In the DRC – and of course also in Gabon and throughout Africa – all that was needed was to let people be. All that was needed was for mendacious, mercenary foreigners to stop exploiting the indigenous inhabitants, to get back on their planes and go back to where they came from, to let people live as they pleased and run their own countries.

Unfortunately, now is now. Schweitzer's simple solution, one by which he lived, is, of course, unattainable. People are not like him.

PART II

The Lambaréné Diary
of Cecil Morris, M.Ch.,
orthopaedic surgeon:

a working visit to Schweitzer's hospital
from 17 May to 3 June 1957

Introduction to the Diary

IN order to keep the hospital functioning well, Schweitzer depended on donors and a turnover of qualified medical and administrative volunteers, a changing guard of professional experts from across the world. While he employed local people, neither funding nor volunteers were forthcoming from the educated stratum of the country itself, nor from its colonial or transitional governments.

In the late 1950s several unconnected events came together within the window of a few years. The air route to Brazzaville had recently launched from Johannesburg's new airport, the biggest in Africa. The South African tycoon and philanthropist Harry Oppenheimer offered travel grants to South African doctors. The country which was to be Gabon, was not yet politically independent of France: from 1960, because of *apartheid*, Gabon would not allow South Africans to enter the country.

My father was one of several successful South African doctors who were invited to work there then, each for just a few weeks at a time.[85] Who Schweitzer's workers and

---

[85] They included Jack Penn, a plastic surgeon and sculptor, who initiated the programme with Harry Oppenheimer's backing; Bobby Roberts, an anaesthetist; Sydney (Joel) Joel-Cohen, a gynaecologist (whose actor-cousin's real name was the same and he took the stage name "Sid James"); Teddy Epstein, an eye surgeon; and in February 1959, George Cohen, a radiologist, who was there at the same time as endocrinologist Raymond "Bill" Hoffenberg. Hoffenberg was soon "banned" by the South African government for his radical politics and left South Africa for Britain. Nicknamed "the physician to the ANC in exile", he was later knighted, and in his last years married a countess.

visitors were, how they financed their sojourns, why they went there and how long they stayed, has barely been documented. The answers would make a fascinating tale.

In the years that followed his tropical experience, my father kept up with Lambaréné hospital matters and while Schweitzer was alive, helped where he could, from a distance. At home, my father was becoming much respected in his field and he went on to have a successful orthopaedic career in South Africa. He was old-school, dedicated to his profession as in days of yore when doctors swore the Hippocratic Oath and were obedient to it for the rest of their lives.

His habit of writing, in his almost illegible, spikey, slanting doctor's hand, executed with a good fountain pen filled with dark blue ink, almost only comprised meticulous medical notes about his patients. On his expedition to Lambaréné he kept a journal, or rather, he made a few notes on flimsy foolscap sheets with, uncharacteristically, a ball-point pen. He stored the pages in a cardboard folder with his professional letterhead printed on the front cover. The familiar dusty-pink wallet is one of the hundreds, even thousands, that neatly packed his consulting rooms' filing cabinets of patients' notes. Fifty years later, some twenty-six years after his death, I opened it.

The contents of the few diary pages are disappointingly meagre, dashed off with my father's typical self-effacement. There is not a thought for posterity. Nevertheless, I was sorry I had ignored them for so long. The pages were surely a rarity that must be preserved, their scribblings shared with the world. A few searches online taught me to calm down. Every second visitor at Schweitzer's humid oasis – medical and managerial volunteers, admirers and critics, philanthropists, journalists, politicians, musicians, photographers, and towards the end of his life, veritable armies of pen-pushing passers-by – all seemed to have made notes, or written an article, or taken a photograph, or had a short book published about their life-changing glimpse into the alternative universe that was Schweitzer's "hospital".

Perhaps I exaggerate - but nobody was neutral about it. Schweitzer's charisma and his strange enterprise in Africa drew a response each time, usually positive – enchanted, amazed, liberated, enthused – but sometimes negative – suspicious, resentful, envious, self-righteous, dismissive, outraged. He had the effect of making every person who met him feel that he had noticed them very particularly. Visitors often felt a need either to confront him aggressively or else to genuflect. Their conviction of his interest in them was not narcissistic or imaginary. Given his brilliance, remarkable memory and playful curiosity, he probably did indeed look hard at those passing through his moral demesne with a watchfulness that, did they but know it, far surpassed their own watchfulness of him.

Initially I thought that some quick and easy research would help make sense of my father's notes. A little reading taught me that publications both by and about Schweitzer are not only numerous but controversial, fraught with medical, political, economic, philosophical and ethical interrogations. Most striking is the difference between the conspicuousness of Schweitzer's name in his lifetime and its rare recognition these days.

What does it mean to be famous, and in particular, famous for one's moral reputation? There is the longevity of Schweitzer's influence simultaneous with its distortion, even decapitation. If a person's fame is begot of the imagination of others, how much does the imaginary correspond to reality? Despite all that has been written about him, so much remains unexplained.

లొ-లి

I was seven years old when my father, a punctilious orthopaedic surgeon in Johannesburg, South Africa, ventured far away for a fortnight to work with Dr Albert Schweitzer in the jungle of central Africa. Because Schweitzer was a "Great Man" who had put aside worldly things in order to serve the needy, in our household his name was always mentioned in a respectful tone.

There was one exception, and it concerned our dog. This was a spritely, snowy-coated Schipperke puppy whom we acquired when my father's departure was imminent. Obviously, we called the dog "Schweitzer" or, the inevitable diminutive, "Schweitzie". My *mittel*-European maternal grandmother would *kvetch* at intervals that she couldn't understand why we had named a white dog "Schwartze". Given where and when we were, it being *apartheid* South Africa, my grandmother's linguistic confusion carried an ironic weight that elicited bitter laughter from adults who overheard her.

My father returned from his equatorial escapade with a pith helmet and the extraordinary story, as I thought then, that it was so hot there that as soon as your shower was over, you were sweating as much as you were beforehand. The shower was in the open air and, as far as I could make out, comprised a bucket of water suspended high up and attached to a string that you pulled to upend it for a single dousing. What's more, the shower included a rain of frogs that lived in the bucket.

Thus it was that at the age of seven, I knew (1) what the legendary Dr Albert Schweitzer looked like because

120

he had written a note to me, in German, in the white space at the bottom of a photograph of himself. In the picture, he is with a baby antelope that looked like Bambi but whom he called Léonie.[86] I knew (2) the approximate location on the map of French Equatorial Africa where was to be found the isolated hospital. It was designated by the nearest town's name, Lambaréné, in what would later be Gabon (which became independent on 17 August 1960). I knew (3) that an honour had been bestowed on my father in his being allowed to work with this venerable personage who seemed to have always been old. He was then eighty-two. Everyone took his physical strength and vitality for granted. I knew (4) that the great doctor lived humbly but not so humbly that he was without a piano encased in lead to protect it from tropical depredation, on which he expertly played Bach. Both the possession of the instrument and the playing of classical music were, in my young mind, contra-indications of deprivation. That he could choose to live most of his life in a steaming jungle amongst lepers, cannibals, pygmies, Bambi and frogs, and continue to play classical works on the piano, signalled to me something both odd and admirable. It still does.

My father was an honest, educated, refined, taciturn white South African. He was deferent to authority, a socially adept introvert, incapable of excess or

---

[86] Why Léonie? I can guess. In 1958-59 Schweitzer was awarded the prestigious Carl Johann Sonning Prize for his outstanding contribution towards European culture. Winston Churchill preceded him in 1950. Until its award to Schweitzer, there had been a long hiatus, possibly owing to legalities concerning the wife of the late Sonning. (The next, biennial, recipients of the prize were Bertrand Russell, and then Niels Bohr.) Sonning's widow subsequently launched the separate Sonning Music Prize, the "Nobel" of the music world. Her name was Léonie Sonning.

extravagance or anything unseemly. He had old-fashioned manners, wore immaculate white shirts with cuff-links, and had perfectly groomed, manly hands with short fingernails. He never went out without two neatly folded white handkerchiefs, one in the breast-pocket of his jacket, one in his trouser-pocket to use. To see a patient, he put on a freshly laundered white medical coat whether he was in his private consulting rooms in the centre of town or at one of the "black" hospitals where he volunteered each week. Notwithstanding his attention to appearances, he was devoid of narcissism. There was a right way and a wrong way to treat a patient, and the right way included wearing a spotless white coat.

In his presence, it was impossible to imagine the gory undertakings of his vocation. He never learnt entirely to hide a wince at the crudity of, say, some less particular visitor's dinner-table joke about the carving of the roast habitually being assigned to my mother when my father must be such an expert himself. Generally, only ingrained politeness curtailed his short fuse, a reputation which served him well in securing peak cooperation in the operating theatre, where he was known to be less polite. If you were his young daughter, you studied hard for exams, you kept quiet during family meals, and you ate up all the horrible green beans on your plate.

Along with the morally impeccable standards of his period and place, he possessed a social and political naivité unremarkable amongst white South Africans during the period of collective insanity that was *apartheid*. He had lived his whole life under the racist legislation that from 1948 the National Party codified as the system of *apartheid*. I recall without pride my own naive, would-be socialist wrangles when I was older, our mutual incomprehension, and the unfortunate distance it

122

put between us. The political time's well-intentioned but benighted way of thinking, or way of not thinking, reveals itself vividly in his Lambaréné notes, as it does in a comparable Eurocentrism, Americentrism or ethnocentrism in the notes of visitors from elsewhere.

My father never breathed a word about it, and he was certainly forewarned, but the insanitary aspects of Schweitzer's hospital must have unsettled him. If his record of his fortnight spent there is meagre, one explanation may be that, constrained by his well-behaved caution, he did not dare utter, let alone commit to paper his reactions to some of the distasteful details that he noticed. It is only since reading accounts of some outspoken visitors that I appreciate the absence of the cosmetic conventions that simply one had to ignore in order to appreciate Schweitzer's achievement.

I have in mind descriptions of the pervasive stench throughout the property in which everything was perpetually moist and rotting until it was consumed by animals or insects; descriptions of the waterless pit latrines for the staff and guests, the carpet of cat, dog, bird, chicken, goat and monkey manure throughout the compound; the open sewer running between the buildings; the bare, mesh-sided accommodations for the three hundred and fifty patients and their often half-naked *gardiens*; the same number of lepers in their nearby village, the sadly repellent appearance of some of those who assisted in the staff and guest accommodations; ambulant patients suffering from grotesque ailments and disfigurements not seen in the West; everywhere the relative poverty. The whole scene, especially viewed from a middle-class, Western perspective, was distressing and shocking.

My fastidious father's notes dwell on remarkably little of all that and just as little on the drama being played out by staff members. There seems to have been a more or less captivating, ongoing tragi-comic soap opera of professional rivalries and private romances, strife that I can't help thinking probably wonderfully mirrored the patients' ethnic wars. My father did not delve. His conservative impulse was always to normalise the extraordinary to the extent of rendering himself oblivious to what was going on in front of his eyes. Add to that his compulsive discretion, even in his private journal, and one senses him constantly neutralising his astonishment.

It surprised me that his dominant refrain in the journal was one that was normally his least concern: food. As a rule, my father ate lightly and sensibly. He had no particular interest in *cuisine* and the cooking at home was plain, healthy and served in small portions. In Lambaréné, he was always hungry. In his notes, I discover a man I don't recognise at all in so far as he is preoccupied with appetite, meals, menus and hunger.

ৡৣ৹

My father's parents had been sophisticated pogrom escapees from eastern Europe, hard-working immigrants who arrived with nothing but their lives in the strange British colony of South Africa. They died young, after scrimping and saving to raise their children well in the wilds of southern Africa, sending their only son to medical school in Cape Town. They had settled in remote Bloemfontein in the middle of the country, in a house that was small enough that, as was not unusual then, their son never slept inside the house. Through all seasons – nights could be searing in summer and freezing in winter – he slept on the open veranda facing the back yard, a swept expanse of hard, dry red earth. Inside the house, there were flawless net curtains on the windows, and an upright piano with gleaming, hinged brass candlesticks either side of the music rack.

It turns out that by his late teenage years, my father had become, coincidentally, since we are concerned with Schweitzer, a concert pianist *manqué*. This fact I discovered only a few years ago on coming upon some notes made by my late great-aunt. Once he had qualified as a doctor, he gave up playing music. He always insisted there be a piano in our house but in my life-time I never heard him play a note. He regularly went to concerts and had a treasured collection of long-playing classical records which he disliked anyone else to touch. No-one asked questions about the old classical music scores in the storage space under the lid that was the piano-stool seat. Silence enveloped what strikes me now as a startling, psychological renunciation. There comes to mind Schweitzer's frequent references to the emotional sustenance he gained from playing the piano or the organ from his earliest years, and I wonder about the psychological effect on my father of his self-inflicted proscription.

I mention these details, much more meaningful with hindsight, because despite the noteworthy parallels of their backgrounds and interests, and despite my father's life-long respect for *le grand docteur,* the two men could not have been more different from each other. My father was as unlikely a candidate as you could wish to find for the mucking in or mucking out that a sojourn at Lambaréné might entail. He was a solid citizen with a life-time of dutiful self-denial behind him but he emanated fastidiousness. He was almost the same age that the charismatic genius Albert Schweitzer had been when he had charmed everyone from Berlin to Barcelona, from modest Lutheran congregations in Strasbourg to aristocrats in Parisian salons, in order to fund his first reckless venture into Africa, to sail into the unknown.

The Lambaréné Diary
of Cecil Morris, M.Ch.,
orthopaedic surgeon:

a working visit to Schweitzer's hospital
from 17 May to 3 June 1957

Friday 17.5.57: Left Jan Smuts U.A.T[87] about half

an hour late due to a faulty switch. Rather nerve-

racking, to taxi all the way back to the start because

there is a fault, especially for an inexperienced

traveller.[88] Looks mighty high up there. Smooth

journey except for a few bumps in the clouds.

---

[87] Jan Smuts Airport, then the biggest airport in Africa, officially opened in October 1953, replacing the old airport at Palmietfontein. Later that month, the French airline U.A.T., using De Havilland Comet aircraft, once the first commercial jet airliner, extended its Paris-Brazzaville route to include Johannesburg. Brazzaville airport was the only one in the region that could handle large aircraft. From there, passengers transferred to smaller planes for onward journeys. These days, in under five hours one can fly the 2792 km/1735 miles between Johannesburg and Brazzaville direct, twice weekly.

[88] Perhaps this was an Air France DC-3. The local nickname for the airline was "Air Chance" because of occasional plane crashes. In the 1930s, the French colonial airline Air Afrique operated sparsely in AEF but after World War II, Air France, UTA and several charter companies provided frequent services.

Touched down at Salisbury — nice airport. Lunch was elegantly served. Passenger next to me, a Mrs Acton[89], nursing sister returning to Borneo.

Arrived at Brazzaville an hour later than I thought we would — had to allow for local time being one hour behind. Pilot compelled to take evasive action at Brazzaville because of an electric storm – further delayed our landing, by quarter to half an hour. At Brazzaville went fairly quickly through Customs.

Raining ++ tropical. Intrigued by Natives talking French.[90] They take a big part in running of country.

---

[89] It's a long shot but she could have been related to Adventist missionary Lionel Acton-Hubbard who then was director of nursing services at the Kwahu mission hospital near Mpraeso in Ghana. He later volunteered with the Red Cross in Biafra and had a long pastoral career in England. Kwahu Hospital had 140 beds and was run by the West African Union Mission until the government nationalised it in 1974.

[90] The diary provides vivid glimpses into *apartheid*'s effect on a white person's reading of his social environment. At the time in southern Africa, "Native" was a supposedly neutral English word used by both black and white people to designate black people. My father would in the past have heard black Africans speak only either English or indigenous languages, including Afrikaans, the South African dialect of Dutch.

Seem capable and courteous. Saw a Native in a uniform drinking a beer at airport bar counter.[91]

Taken by U.A.T. van to Hotel [des] Relais Aériens. Pleasant place. Built for tropics. Scattered buildings. Dining room altogether open on one side, can't be closed. All mosaic flooring. Bedrooms large, on same floor, about 25 x 15. In one corner – an aluminium structure contains toilet, basin, bidet, lavatory and a shower.

Dinner about 9 p.m. Sat with an English girl, Miss Markmann, also going to Lambaréné.

Saturday 18/5/57: Left in Air France [aeroplane]. Again a delay, one and a half hours, due to an oil leak in a prop. Three stops, at Djambala, Franceville, and Lastoursville, all on turf runways.[92]

---

[91] There were strict alcohol prohibitions in South Africa then. Alcohol, like sex, was associated with all the licentiousness that a strict Calvinist state could muster. It was illegal, for instance, for a woman to enter a bar unless it was "a Ladies' Bar". My father had possibly never yet seen a black person in Africa drink alcohol amongst whites albeit that we had lived for two years in Britain, when he was studying for his M.Ch. in London and Edinburgh, 1952-1954.

[92] As the crow flies, Lambaréné is only 400 miles from Brazzaville but the planes made detours to stop elsewhere *en route*. Ava Helen Pauling records in her 1959 journal that their

These places are mainly mission stations.

Interesting feature is that all colours travel on plane.

Native on adjacent seat: his family drank beer on the plane.

This journey is an adventure.

From Lastoursville to Lambaréné, practically only dense jungle. Miles and miles south, no gap whatsoever. Landed at Lambaréné, met by Sister [Albertine]Van [Beeck] Vollenhoven, a Hollander.[93]

Then taken by camion to river, where piroque waiting for us. River crossing takes nearly three quarters of

---

plane made a detour to "Bitan" (she means Bitam) to pick up a patient on a stretcher. Bitam is in the extreme north near the Cameroon border.

[93] With the title "Sister" he may be honouring her nursing status, not indicating a religious order. She had charge of the psychiatric ward, was about 29, and "tall, slender, attractive, intelligent, compassionate" (Cousins (1960), p.144), green-eyed, and "sophisticated". Clara Urquhart said she had "deep intelligence" and in her free time played the lyre. In a letter from Günsbach to Dr van der Kreek in Lambaréné (23 August 1955), Schweitzer wrote that she would find in Miss van Beeck-Vollenhoven "a good comrade: she is a little deaf, but it does not weaken her much" and she would suit the hospital. She would depart for Africa "with Foucauld on September 30 if she gets a cabin." She worked at Lambaréné from 18 October 1955 to 16 May 1958. An Albertine van Vollenhoven co-authored a book in 1988 about an anthroposophical approach to home nursing. While the van Vollenhovens married into the Dutch Royal family, the name is better known through D. H. Th. Vollenhoven, the Dutch philosopher.

an hour. As hospital is approached, rowers start to send calls over the water: two notes, one ? on inspiration.

Then see all come down to water. Schweitzer too. Hospitable welcome. Schweitzer very genial and kind looking. Margaret [van der Kreek][94] there with a Dr Friedman[95], long moustache. Weather not too hot. Very humid, perspiration ++. Given lunch.

Taken around hospital by M[argaret]. Very primitive indeed. Theatre — wooden floor. Wards

---

[94] Margaret van der Kreek, who could not have been thirty, was Schweitzer's chief surgeon. When I was a child, I took her to be a nurse when she visited us in Johannesburg. Her reserved demeanour stilled us all. Clara Urquhart – and others – remarked upon her classic beauty and her "poetic quality". Norman Cousins devotes some time to describing his conversations with her (Cousins, pp. 68ff). My father may have first met her through surgeon Jack Penn when she visited Johannesburg in February 1957 to study new reconstructive surgery techniques. She worked at the Lambaréné hospital from 9 March 1955 to 14 July 1958, 6 March 1959 to 15 August 1960, and 13 October 1970 to 6 June 1971. The last dates were after Schweitzer died.

[95] Dr Richard Friedmann (described both as Hungarian and Czech) was Schweitzer's taciturn and permanent senior physician. Friedmann had a number tattooed on his arm, designating the concentration camp in which he had been incarcerated by the Nazis during World War II. He had survived but not his family. He first visited Lambaréné from Israel around 1954, not intending to stay long. He worked there from 9 October 1956 to 10 May 1962, and from 14 April 1963 to 31 January 1969, i.e. he remained after Schweitzer died.

have wooden bunks, wives sleep on floor next to husband, even vice versa. Wards dark, painted black. Apparently the principle is that this will hide dirt. The time of the staff is occupied with other duties[96].

Cooking is also done on side of ward. Supplies are provided but patients prefer to prepare their own food. New principle in newer wards is to have bedroom on one side, then a street[97], and opposite side of the road a kitchen. There are 350 patients but with families there must be about a thousand people in the hospital village[98].

---

[96] He is implying that they don't have time to wash the walls. Goldwyn mentions that every Thursday afternoon "the operating room and the wards are scoured with some strong soap" and that after each operation the patient's family "usually" cleaned the operating room (14 and 27 November 1960).

[97] "Street" was the term used at the hospital. In fact, it was an unpaved path running between the buildings.

[98] He was quick to realise, probably because of early conversations with Margaret van der Kreek, that Schweitzer's great achievement was not so much to have built a "hospital" as an indigenous village with a medical facility. For Augustin Emane's ground-breaking research (*op. cit.*) over eight years, he interviewed about sixty Gabonese former patients or those who had accompanied patients to the hospital. Emane reports that in their over-riding sense of the precariousness of life, Schweitzer's "hospital" was understood to be a place of temporary protective refuge, a healing encampment where could be found a brief suspension of life's uncertainty. Unlike critics of the West who must fix their manichean images of Schweitzer for or against him, Emane found that local people

In meeting the staff, both black and white, one

must shake hands with everybody[99]. Hospital

language is French, but staff speak mainly German.

Having difficulty with contacting Schweitzer. His

German different to mine! Actually is Alsace.

I am struck by the management of the place. It is

run by so few, even as regards the medical staff.[100]

Believe Schweitzer feels too many will complicate

---

perceived him without judgement, "in the moment", according
to the present word, the palaver.

[99] In *apartheid* South Africa, black and white adults rarely
touched and certainly did not greet each other by shaking hands.
Apartheid legislation attempted to suppress the neurotic threat
of unbridled desire. The outcome, obviously, was a nation of
slightly paranoid, aggressive people. Dr George Cohen (in
conversation, *op. cit.*) remembered Schweitzer saying to him,
"There are two things that give me jaundice. One is trying to
grow cacao plants and the other is the South African
government." Dr Cohen was at Lambaréné in February 1959,
six months after Verwoerd, the architect of *apartheid*, had
become president of South Africa.

[100] Three years later, Dr Goldwyn makes a similar observation.
While he cannot praise highly enough the fearlessness and
dedication of the staff, he notes: "We could have better care [of
the patients] if we had more nurses." According to Brabazon
(p.457), by the end, both the infrastructure of the buildings and
the number of patients had grown far too large for the aging
Schweitzer to manage as well as he had done once. The number
of patients treated rose from 3800 in 1958 to 6500 in 1963. In
1962, 802 operations were performed; in 1963, 950.

matters.[101] ? Not more than twenty helpers.

The natives eat bananas (enormous size), manioc ([cassava] root prepared with leaves banana ? leaves around it) and other fruit. Eat fish if they can get it. Meat is practically *non est*. Only seem to be the odd goats in the area.

The meals here are very austere: prayers are said at lunch and supper, with a hymn as well at night meals. Breakfast is bread, dinkel[102] or other kind of cake, jam and tea, coffee, cocoa. Lunch also not much more. Various bits and pieces, paw paw, sweet potato,

---

[101] The remark has poignancy in hindsight. As we saw in Part I, after Schweitzer's death in 1965, when his daughter and her husband took over the management, they rebuilt it as a modern hospital with plumbing, electricity, and more staff. Schweitzer's original hospital was preserved to entertain tourists. Medical services improved initially but after a few years, materials and funds routinely vanished. By then, Rhena Schweitzer-Miller and her husband had left the country.

[102] *Dinkel* is spelt. Compared to ordinary wheat it allows a slower starch metabolism, has lower glutamic acid levels and better proteins. It is thus suitable for diabetics and those with sensitive intestines. Schweitzer, who had suffered from dysentery and then bowel complications in his 40s, ate intelligently. In the 1920s, Dr Max Gerson supposedly cured Hélène Schweitzer's tuberculosis using his "dietary therapy". Gerson also claimed that Schweitzer had Type II diabetes which his dietary therapy cured.

marrow, bread, tea, etc. Not much more at night.

Sunday dinner had stewed goat (special) and once

cold gelatine soup[103]. Breadfruit balls, *pomme de*

cythère as a sweet.

I feel perpetually hungry. Have no doubt will lose

weight.[104]

Use of palm oil with salads.[105] To me it is rather

unwholesome.

---

[103] My father could barely make himself a cup of tea let alone de-code a recipe. He must have meant cold *consommé,* or, more exactly, gelatinous cold bone broth or meat stock, a dish with amino acids, good for intestinal problems (cf. fn.101).

[104] Dr George Cohen observed that everyone at the hospital (in February 1959) was given a bunch of bananas every day. He remarked to a staff member that meat was never on the menu. At the very next meal, there was meat: crocodile meat. He told me this story not in order to discuss menus but to illustrate that Schweitzer micro-managed and had "spies" who loyally reported back to him. Separately, Schweitzer wrote about the vivid difference in personality and energy levels of local people compared to Nigerian immigrant labourers and wondered if that could be attributed to their differential protein intake. Fish was not a local staple although most people lived near rivers. During her week-long visit with her husband Linus, Ava Helen Pauling writes (23 July 1959): "Roasted peanuts for dessert tonight. How everyone loved them. There is a protein deficiency here almost certainly – especially for these hard-working nurses! I must send nuts."

[105] From the earliest days of his arrival in the region, Schweitzer questioned why production of palm oil was not widespread (Urquhart, p.41). He did not live to discover the calamity associated with his query, that today half our food and cosmetics contain "Conflict Palm Oil" and that its production

Had once a real pang of hunger, with cramps and nausea.[106] I think this is why I was told I have bitten off more than I can chew!

Can drink a fair amount of mandarin (*naartjie*) juice.

The total calorie content is inadequate, and the protein deficiency is, I think, great.

The nurses wear white dresses, with a sort of pinafore arrangement over it while at work. White stockings are worn to below-knee height.[107] Looking at these girls, given the impression that they are wearing habits. In fact, I consider that their work here is a kind of dedication to a service, much like nuns do. They live only for their work. Some are so devoted that they will take very sick children into

---

cannot be separated from human exploitation and ecological devastation worldwide. See Diary entry for 30 May 1957.

[106] Three years later, Dr Goldwyn describes the hospital food as "abundant and tasty". He found, he said, contrary to lore discouraging eating much in hot weather, that one felt weak if one didn't eat a lot. Amongst the local people, "If children do not eat, mothers say, 'The crocodile is coming.' They eat." (15, 18 November 1960.)

[107] Staff were encouraged to wear white for reasons of hygiene, to deter insects, and presumably too, to make life easier for the laundry workers.

their bedrooms at night. They are the quintessence of kindness to their patients. They greet their patients all the time with a sweet peculiar lilt in their voices.

The greeting is "Bonsoir" at all hours of the day. This greeting seems to be derived from the natives, and the voice inflection is the same as the natives greet them.

Schweitzer frowns on his staff going to Lambaréné [town] when off duties. One of the reasons is the risk in the piroques and also probably the fact that the feeling of dedication to service is not compatible with cavorting around the town.

Incidentally Schweitzer objects to outboard motors on boats. He is worried about the sandbanks but also feels that the speed is not required in his relationship to the outside world. I personally feel very upset to see the three paddlers working to propel the cumbersome piroque for three quarters of an hour.

The feeling of dedication also applies to the Medical staff. They very seldom leave the place.

I understand that from time to time, there have been incompatibles[108] on the staff who really do not understand what Schweitzer has built up and what he has worked for. Those people, with good intentions, probably want to change the place into a more modern hospital. It is not realized that the nomenclature "Hospital" is incorrect and the real intention is an out-patient service with facilities for the odd emergencies. Although there are so-called beds, this is really a board and lodging facility. The patient must have a "guardienne" with him or her, that is, a spouse. The patient must also contribute a fee towards his treatment. For an operation it is usually 500 Eq. Francs, about £1. For a consultation, 2000-300 Fr. The fee however is not insisted on if the patient cannot pay. So it has to be understood that this is not really a hospital.[109]

---

[108] A wry euphemism typical of my father, as is his frequent use of the passive voice. Even in private jottings such as these, he minded his language.

[109] My father assumes that hospital health-care is by definition state-funded, "free" for patients, as was the case at the time in South Africa. Schweitzer found that he had to charge for pills, even a token fee, because people liked the idea of taking pills

Personal feelings and personality factors frequently result in tiffs among the staff.[110] This must be expected because they live together for twenty-four hours of the day, every day. At first I thought that some of the helpers could be classed as saints, but getting to know them must invite the phrase, "There are no Saints".[111]

I am given to understand that the heat is a potent factor in the fights among the staff. After the hot wet season, things can be trying and the staff can become particularly fatigued. This leads to one becoming on

---

even if they didn't need them and he needed a way of deterring them. "Patients like the doctor who gives pills and often a family will feign illness to stay on so that they can get a food ration as well." (Goldwyn, 5 November 1960.)

[110] Over three years later Dr Goldwyn made his private list of things that would improve the hospital, and one of them was "Less petty politics amongst staff". "I feel that *esprit de corps* is sorely lacking. In the long run it is more detrimental to the care of patients than an ignorance of a particular technique." (14 November and 2 December 1960)

[111] When I spoke to him in 2016, Dr George Cohen applied the same phrase to Schweitzer. "He was no saint," said Dr Cohen. He was authoritarian in manner, liked to talk, not listen. He was "not a very good doctor". By the last, Dr Cohen was referring to his dismay that patients diagnosed with advanced cancer were let go without treatment. Dr Goldwyn introduces an alternative interpretation. A staff member told him never to tell a patient that she is terminally ill: "The tribe may harm her if they think she is 'doomed to die'."

edge, and more liable therefore to "flare up" for insignificant reasons.[112]

On Sunday afternoon went by piroque to Lambaréné with Dr Byron Bernard an American Zoologist here. He has brought milk goats from the Cincinnati Zoo for Schweitzer. He went to see if his lorry was OK. In typical American style, "Milk Goats for Dr Schweitzer" was painted on his lorry.[113]

---

[112] My father is typically economical with detail, here about the quarrels amongst staff members. Goldwyn is more illuminating when he writes that he was appalled to discover that there was staff gossip that he, a happily married man, was having an affair with another volunteer, probably simply because they were both Americans and talked to each other a lot. She was Marie-Louise Cullum (possibly of Alabama, later of St Thomas, Virgin Islands) – whom he described elsewhere as religious and modest. He wrote in his journal: "Here everybody is so worried about his own sexuality that he or she displaces their desires on others. This aspect of Lambaréné is detestable and it is a shame that with Dr. Schweitzer as a symbol it occurs here and cheapens life here." (25 November 1960)

[113] In *Hearts from Heaven: Love from the Afterlife* (Inspiring Voices, 2014), ch.4, Leatrice L. Marson records that Schweitzer needed help in reversing the calcium deficiency of his patients. In 1957, "Dr Byron Bernard [1917- 2006], a zoologist, started a project called Goats for Schweitzer, which became a documentary film series." Her husband, the late Robert James Marson, was Director of Overseas Operations for "a large pharmaceutical company". He authorised a "multimillion-dollar donation of medicine to the project, which saved many lives. The project asked for the donation in exchange for publicity, but the company preferred to keep this purely a private donation." An obituary about Dr Bernard in the *Cincinnatti Post* (19 August 2006) puts the value of the pharmaceutical supplies

140

Visited the Chef d'District and his wife at their

home because Dr B wanted to fix up his permit to

take baby gorilla Penelope back to the States.[114]

Lambaréné, i.e. the town itself, is situated on an

island in the Ogowe river. Not a particularly beautiful

place. Poor roads and I think poor people i.e.

financially.

Monday 20/5/57: Saw some patients in the

consultation clinics. These are held Mondays,

---

at a more credible $20,000, and seventeen as the number of
Nubian milk goats whose transport Dr Bernard supervised. In
The Cincinnati Zoo and Botanical Garden (Arcadia, 2010), Joy
W. Kraft records that the goats were a gift from Fred Knoop of
the American Dairy Goat Association. Fifteen of them were
delivered in a four-wheel drive Studebaker by Dr Bernard and
his colleague Cathryn Hosea Hilker, an expert on cheetahs. (My
father doesn't mention her.) Dr Bernard was familiar with
Africa because after World War II he had facilitated hunting
groups to find wild animals to re-stock depleted European zoos.
[114] While my father was at the hospital, Dr Bernard departed
with Schweitzer's gift for Cincinnatti in exchange for the milk
goats and medical supplies. The gift was the three-year old
gorilla Penelope. Before going to the Cincinnatti Zoo, she lived
with Dr Bernard and his family, as one of the children, for three
years. She died at the Zoo – by my own calculation not on the
date of the publication of the first obituary, as is often stated,
but – on 27 April 1989. She was 35, then the oldest lowland
gorilla in the Zoo. She was the first gorilla in the world to give
birth to four offspring while in captivity. She had become the
mate of the Zoo's "most popular" gorilla, King Tut, and was
survived by her four children, thirteen grandchildren and two
great-grandchildren.

Wednesdays and Fridays; Tuesdays, Thursdays and Saturdays are reserved for operations.

Did a Ward Round with Doctoresse, as Margaret is called. Amazed at the number of inguinal hernia cases, both in males and females, predominantly in the males of course. One of the etiological factors given is that the natives here are riddled with G.C.[115] [gonorrhea] and get urethral strictures, thus producing the herniae by excessive straining at micturition.

Saw also many cases of elephantiasis of scrotums and legs, really monstrous and hideous. In ward round was shown the famous case of drilling of exposed tibia in order to produce a granulation tissue

---

[115] Robert Goldwyn writes: "Patients say they have a venereal disease to get an injection but usually they do have it. We seldom treat partners; the male will often bring in 4 women. Natives buy wives; a man likes to marry a woman with daughters. He gets money when they are married." "The price for a wife . . . is between $15 and $100 – more for someone with children because she has proven fertility. Tribe members do not help others in tasks especially caring for children. If a child gets a fever during the night, they will feel that a curse has been cast by the other tribe members. As Dr. Schweitzer has written, Africans are not happy – they are continuously disturbed by curses, evil spirits, etc." (5, 12, 13 November 1960.)

which could later be skin grafted. The reason for non-amputation is that there is a good stump to the end of the leg. I personally have my doubts and I have recommended an amputation; through the knee is best, and then to be supplied with a peg-leg.

In the consultation I was asked to see a spastic paralysis of birth cerebral palsy; supraspinatus tendonitis which I injected with hydrocortone; syphilitic myositis of an upper extremity with skin contraction of anterior axillary fold and stiff elbow. In this case I did not suggest further surgery because of the extensive tissue-paper scarring which would not take much surgical handling.

A visit was paid to the Leper Village. Nurse Trudi is in charge.[116] Extremely devoted to her work and

---

[116] Young Swiss Trudi Bochsler had charge of the expanding leper village for the periods 14 December 1950 to 27 May 1952 and 7 April 1956 to 11 August 1958. An awed Urquhart describes her as "the very essence of dedication", "dressing the patients' often frightful sores". She'd argue with Schweitzer as few others dared, in order to get a larger share of facilities for "her" lepers. In May 1952, she left to study leprosy in Switzerland. Using his Nobel Peace Prize money, Schweitzer began planning a separate leprosarium to be built a short walk from the main compound. When my father met her in 1957, Nurse Trudi was back, running the new leper village. She later

her patients, so much so that she must watch out that she does not catch leprosy.[117] I was amazed at the number of cases which showed sinuses of the feet. Got the impression that these were ordinary sinuses which would not heal because of being rigid walled cavities. Advised saucerizing the soft tissue sinuses and plugging CVG [with vaseline gauze]. Suggestion accepted.

Was told that sulphones are wonderful for maculo-papular lesions, but made no impression on sinuses. For this reason, thought of laying open the sinuses. However, have my doubts about my suggestion because there is most probably an underlying bone lesion, and personally I can't feel keen to submit these cases to extensive surgery. They are after all fundamentally nerve diseases. One wonders how the

---

left to marry a doctor whom she had met at the hospital. Dr Isao Takahashi from Japan took over for the periods 24 December 1958 to 26 July 1961, 8 October 1961 to 12 July 1965, December 1965 to 25 May 1966. It was said that he returned to Japan because of ill-health. He went on to establish a formidable medical reputation.

[117] Goldwyn was urged not to keep a drum that he had bought that had been made by a very ill leper. "The transmissibility of the disease has not been definitely established." (12 November 1960.)

full blown Winnet-Orr[118] method would do. I personally will leave alone.

Asked later in the day to see a suppurative myositis. Two lesions, one in thigh non-suppurative, and one in buttock suppurative, and giving a beautiful Trendelenburg gait. Performed also a partial amputation of a thumb.

Tuesday [21/5/57]: Helped M. do a few hernia cases. I am being useful because Dr Catchford[119] is ill, and my presence as an assistant is required. They do the typical Bassini operation. These hernias are large, having large sac protrusions.

Later in the day, I did a compound fracture of the metatarsals due to an axe wound. Because of the nearby plantations, axe wounds are common. This patient had cleft the forefoot in two between the 2nd and 3rd metatarsals.

The plantations are finding great difficulty in obtaining Native labour. The reason is that two years

---

[118] Winnet-Orr was an American orthopaedic surgeon who invented this surgical method to treat bone infections. – David Hirschowitz.

[119] He means Dr Frank Catchpool.

145

ago, the local natives were granted citizenship, and cannot therefore be compelled to work. Before, labour was conscripted from each village. Labour has now to be imported from Nigeria (these latter Natives speak English).

Schweitzer does not favour this liberal view. Presumably he regards this as premature. He also does not like the fact that alcohol is now freely obtainable by them.

The local Natives to me look unhealthy, unexciting and devoid of any inherent personality. Compared to the South African Native, they lack a vitality and colour in their behaviour. Their clothing is drab. The women wear an old piece of material around them, and their sitting position is indecently amusing. They sit with their legs wide open, but a small flap of material is made to hang down the pubic region to hide their pubis. The women are sold by the head of the family who may be an aged uncle or aunt, and if the husband is not satisfied, the women are recalled to their home. The price demanded is never apparently fixed.

Wednesday 22/5/57: Attended consultations. Later in afternoon did three cases of Lepers at the Leper Village. There was a bit of a difference between Trudi and M. about where the ops should be done, in the Village or in the [operating] theatre. Trudi wanted them done in the Village. She said she has difficulty persuading her patients to go to the operating theatre. Schweitzer was brought into the argument but of course I kept out of the argument. Eventually the operations were done at the Village.

Schweitzer came along to watch. The procedures were of course kept minor.

Thursday [23/5/57]: Did my first cold operation here — stabilisation of an equino-varus[120] deformity due to an old compound fracture of the left foot.

The usual procedure of scrubbing is to do one scrub before the first case, and then simply change gloves and gown for the following cases. In my case, just before I was to do it, we all went down to the river to say farewell to Mme Schweitzer who was returning

---

[120] Congenital *talipes equinovarus*, CTEV or "club foot", was one of my father's areas of expertise.

147

to Europe.[121] We then returned to the theatre to do my case, and as per custom, simply changed gown and gloves!

I was amazed that there was no choral farewell to Mme S by Natives. They were emotionless.

This departure of Mme Schweitzer was rather sad. In the opinion of many, this will be her last voyage. She is very ill due to a cardiac condition with cerebral arteriosclerosis.[122] I did not meet her but very interesting information was imparted to me. I was amazed to hear that she was fully Jewish in origin. She apparently had a lot to do with the building up of the hospital and the running of it afterwards. It is said that the idea of the hospital is mainly hers. I was also told that many of his philosophical thoughts are really the combined efforts of both him and her.

She always used to sit up with him late at night while he was working. She was known to be very

---

[121] He is describing events of the day before. Hélène Schweitzer (1879-1957) left Lambaréné on Wednesday 22nd May 1957.
[122] Also known as vascular dementia. I've not seen it mentioned but perhaps the condition partly explained her years of irascible behaviour.

brilliant in her early days, getting the Ph.D. degree in about 1902, which for a woman then, much have been outstanding.[123]

The orthopaedic part of this hospital is primitive and must remain so under the present system. Asepsis is really practically useless to try to maintain. General anaesthesia which is so important to us, is so poor that nothing further need be said.[124] The Ombredanne bomb[125] is used with ether anaesthesia. Evipan[126] was given for my case, but

---

[123] Aside from her medical diagnosis, little of what my father was told about "Mme Schweitzer" is accurate. (See the biographical summary in Chapter 2 above.) Perhaps he was told a story that was trotted out for visitors and that Schweitzer either had not overheard, which is unlikely, or chose not to set straight. Schweitzer assiduously refrained from undermining Hélène publicly, a habit that she did not reciprocate. She always had been a keen attendee of university lectures but did not have a degree. She had been a language teacher and social worker when she completed a course in nursing before accompanying Schweitzer to Africa in 1913.

[124] Three years later, the anaesthesia facilities were no better, as noted by Goldwyn: "Anaesthesia here is either too light or too deep. I have controlled myself fairly well (from expressing any criticism). Postoperative mortality 4 of 450 patients and 85 'accidents' recorded from June '59 to June '60." (3 and 12 November 1960.)

[125] Ombredanne: an anaesthetic inhaler, French, 1906. – David Hirschowitz.

[126] Evipan: a barbiturate used to induce anaesthesia in the 1940s and 50s. – David Hirschowitz.

given so slowly that the patient was able to detoxicate it while it was still being given.

I am truly amazed at the paucity of orthopaedic cases. I have not seen a case of skeletal T.B. although there is a ward here of pulmonary T.B. Poliomyelitis is present but only to a minor degree, and the cases seen were mainly adults who have had the paralysis for many years. Trauma is also not in any great frequency. Presumably when the plantations were in full swing, trauma must have been plentiful. I also have not seen much in the congenital sphere, only one case of C.T.E.V.[127] in a 3/52 babe brought by Dr Weismeyer[128], the Government doctor from Lambarene. Generally speaking, in a hospital of this size, orthopaedic cases are practically *non est*.

Friday 24/5/57: Paid a visit to Lambarene with Dr Byron Bernard, veterinary surgeon, Cincinnati Zoo, to organize his truck over to the hospital. Had a cold beer at a club "Le Circle". This was made only of wood and bamboo, and all open. Very cool in this. Then

---

[127] Congenital *talipes equinovarus*.
[128] He means Dr Weissberg.

decided in view of late hour for lunch at hospital, to have lunch at a club in the town. Really enjoyed this meal. Was a wonderful change. Had some *hors d'oevres* like a polony, then beef, and an apple followed by cheese (all sorts) and coffee. Meal of course accompanied by *vin rouge*, and lastly cognac. At same table was a Mr Sebior, whose wife is an actress in Paris (?D'Alleman).[129] Pleasant company. Felt very good, and then we drove off to the ferry. En route, hit a horizontal branch and knocked off the platform on top of the cab of the truck. This platform had been made too high. Quite a job to put it back. Arranged to have it repaired. I returned to the hospital, getting a lift in a motor boat.

Saturday: [25/5/57]: Assisted at operations.

Sunday [26/5/57]: Listened to music. The food over the weekend is interesting. Saturday night consists of cocoa, bread and cheese, and butter. Sunday midday is the "big" meal. This week was

---

[129] He is suggesting that the wife, or the couple, is German, not French.

chicken, last week goat. Sunday night, the old routine, bread, butter, jam.

Monday [27/5/57]: Had the best meal ever at this place at lunch time. First pawpaw, then chicken puree served in shells — really delicious. This was followed by a dish of rice, eggs with mayonnaise and a salad of egg fruit, green peppers and tomato. For sweets, some chocolate pudding. Really enjoyed this meal, I think my first one. Dr Schweitzer even offered me half his chopped pineapple. He eats all bits and pieces, lettuce, fried egg plant, odd egg, prunes, other diced vegetables.

Saw some cases in consultation, particularly two with reference to amputation. Discussed with Schweitzer. One, a severe elephantiasis, he favoured conservative treatment. Trying out injection of cortisone locally at the margin of the oedema + elevation. The other, the famous drilling case to stimulate granulation tissue, he agreed that I should amputate.

The nursing staff to me look very "ratty" these

days. M says it is the end of the hot season and this is trying for them. Also some are due for leave after completing their contracts. Their nerves are on edge and they want things their own way. Consider the discussion we had about amputating the leg of the case mentioned above. The nurse flared up when the possibility of delaying the amputation was mentioned.

Tuesday 28/5/57: Did two ops, a Lambrinudi stabilization[130] and the amputation. Both went off well. Actually was filmed while operating by Dr. B.[131] The theatres here are not enclosed. They are open practically all round but covered in by gauze wire. The operations can be viewed by all passers-by.

The theatre floor consists of wood flooring. The organization in the theatre is good. While the operated case is carried away, the next one is brought in and placed on the other theatre table to be subsequently wheeled into position. The lighting is

---

[130] A surgical procedure to correct drop-foot, flail foot and club-foot.
[131] Dr Byron Bernard.

good and the generator has to be switched on whenever an operation is in progress.

When not busy, one gets really bored. It is also difficult to do any systematic reading. It must be the weather which does not allow this. One is in a perpetual sweat. Strangely enough, one doesn't smell. I think the perpetual sweating is in a sense self-cleansing.

Notwithstanding the heat, one must keep all the time active in order to retain your sanity. One is too uncomfortable doing nothing. The days I am not operating are really trying.

I notice that Dr Schweitzer is always on the go. He is always doing something.[132] Most of the time he probably spends building things here and there, but at present he is re-organising the pharmacy. He is re-

---

[132] Many observers remarked upon Schweitzer's exceptional powers of concentration and that he was always constructively busy. Dr Goldwyn writes in 1960, "He works continuously. . . (His) attention to detail is fantastic." Schweitzer was then 85. Marion Preminger (1957) notes that Schweitzer spent their 18-day Europe-bound voyage "locked up" in his cabin, writing. When they disembarked, the purser told him that he had worked harder than anyone on the boat, "except for the barber".

labelling the drugs in French and German.[133] All is written in his own hand. He is extremely systematic in everything he does. His evenings are spent attending to his voluminous correspondence, and in the early mornings, he practices the piano.[134]

After dinner, Dr Schweitzer stayed behind because it was raining and he spoke about the atom bomb. He felt he was able to speak to the world about this as he was not involved in any politics. He also told me that in South Africa there has been a 100% increase of radioactivity since the explosion of H-bomb on Christmas Island.[135] A poem read by Schweitzer — this was sent to him by a German girl.

---

[133] "Pfizer and others send him old drugs that are out of date when they reach him so Pfizer can deduct it from income taxes. They often get the throw-aways. Dr. Schweitzer, however, is humbly grateful for them, although I think this is shameful – like a philanthropist today giving away Confederate money." (Goldwyn, 25 November 1960.)

[134] Before it was sent, Schweitzer's friends had had it encased in lead to protect it from the climate's depredations and had fitted it with a pedal keyboard to simulate his preferred musical instrument, the organ. Goldwyn observed that there were two pianos in the dining room, one old and one new, and Schweitzer used the old one. (7 November 1960.)

[135] The British thermonuclear weapons programme to develop the megaton hydrogen bomb began in December 1954. Nuclear tests were conducted over Christmas Island and also 400 miles

The rainy season continues. It is hot and humid.
The weather is quite wrong. Everybody says that the
dry season should have commenced mid-May.[136]

Wednesday [29/5/57] : Went over to Lambarene.
Booked air passage. Had lunch at the old hotel with
Mon. Jacques Sebior and wife, and the American.
Returned by piroque.

Heard that I am booked for Sabena flight.

Thursday [30/5/57]: Ascension Day, and
therefore a public holiday. Went for lunch at
Lambarene at Dr and Mme Weissberg's house.[137]
Taken over the hospital on the island. Very
disappointed at what I saw. The hospital, like

---

south, over Malden Island. The first British H-bomb was
dropped on 15 May 1957 and tests ended on 11 September
1958. The H-bomb series was given the codename Operation
Grapple, symbolizing the four-pointed grappling hook of inter-
service cooperation between the three armed services and the
recently created Atomic Weapons Research Establishment
under the directorship of Sir William Penney.

[136] Metereologists at the time of the bomb tests noted an effect
on Amazonian rainfall. It isn't clear whether my father means to
associate the tests with the effect on African equatorial rainfall.

[137] At the end of the Pauling's visit two years later, Ava Helen
Pauling notes (Friday 24 July 1959): "Dr Weissberg and his
wife. She paints – rather badly. Their house is fine and they had
two lovely ivory carvings of antelope – exquisite. View
magnificent from their hilltop house."

Schweitzer's, is only an apology for a hospital. The place is dirty, with practically no nursing at all. The local authorities obviously don't care much for the Natives. Dr Weissberg is the only doctor there. The medicine of necessity must be primitive because there is no money allocated to hospitals. I think the figure mentioned was £1m francs per year (AEF francs).[138] It makes one feel that South Africa's effort for the natives is superb.[139] Returned to this hospital in a "Rapide" with Gen. de Gaulle's nephew. Unfortunately could not go on to the palm plantation which he is running – about one hour's run from here.

---

[138] This was before Gabon's independence which came in August 1960. In 1962, a sceptical journalist, Roman Brodmann, arrived with "the usual prejudices". In his article, *Die Wahrheit über Lambaréné,* he describes how dirty the government hospital is and the inadequately equipped operating theatre. There is no second doctor "to assist at any operation that presents any difficulty. So the doctor sends cases that are at all complicated across the river to Schweitzer's hospital. I found nearly half the beds unoccupied at the government hospital; Schweitzer's hospital is full to overflowing and being expanded all the time." (Translated in Brabazon (1975), p.458.)

[139] Owing to an inexplicable irony, during the *apartheid* era in South Africa, it was begrudgingly acknowledged internationally that the country had the best state-funded, urban hospitals in Africa serving the segregated black population. This was in contrast of course to the so-called Bantustans, where the apartheid government – criminally – provided almost no medical facilities.

I understand that it is hoped that this palm plantation will supply all French soap manufacturers with the palm oil they need.

Yesterday at consultation in the afternoon, Dr Weissberg brought two cases, one an old polio for caliper measurement and the other a club foot which I showed him how to plaster. Then someone came along for medical advice, bringing a cock in a beautifully made round crate of horizontal bars of bamboo and the sides made of a criss-cross of strips of leaves, as his consultation fee. During the history taking, the tribute constantly crowed loudly.

Friday 31/5/57: Very interested in results of the leper cases which were operated upon. The lesions now seem to be granulating well from the bottom and they look relatively clean.

The treatment of cases with chronic leg ulcers — we would call them "veld sores" — seems to be very promising following the use of hydrocortisone [?]

(Hydroptic – [Merck] Sharp and Dohme[140])

opthalmic emulsion locally. They do look clean and

epithelializing well. Other interesting facets in the

treatment of cases is the use of ordinary zinc oxide

ointment to prevent irritation of the skin (? should

use this for dermatitis in the case of osteomyelitis

after V.G.[vaseline gauze] and P.O.P. [plaster of

Paris]).

Saw a case of Frambesia[141] of wrist and thigh, in a

young girl. Typical signs of syphilitic lesion: round,

rolled, everted edges.

Mention should be made of the extensive use in

the hospital of bamboo sticks tipped with cotton wool

in all cases, both of application of antiseptic

(mercurochrome "range") and in the exploration of a

sinus. The latter procedure is I think bad because it

just seems to enlarge the sinus and give it depth, so

promoting a rigid walled cavity.

---

[140] MSD: a German drug company established in 1851.– David
Hirschowitz.
[141] Also known as yaws. The condition, which resembles
leprosy and syphilis, is highly infectious, being transmitted by
direct contact.

At the post office in Lambarene today: went over in a piroque oared by Kalomutoo. Sent two telegrams and the procedure took a full half hour. I was attended at first by one black official, and a big discussion was held as to the number of words. Then the second and more senior official came and took over. He knew his job, but did everything at a slow pace. If I did not have plenty of time on my hands, it could have been very irritating. His face was totally expressionless with clenching of the jaw and contraction of his masseter muscles taking place. He was obviously aware of his position. Also, when he had to find change for me, he remained completely without any feeling in the matter. He took his time getting change. It may be that this is his attitude to the white man. There is probably a lot to be said for the South African way. Our standard of efficiency remains very high both in the white and the black, compared to the local situation in A.E.F. A very important factor comes to my mind in that in South Africa, the white man has come to stay. It is his permanent home, whereas in these African colonies, the white man individually is very temporary, and therefore he doesn't care if the post official is incompetent. In fact, he doesn't even go to the Post Office because he sends one of his numerous black servants to transact his business there. He does not therefore notice this pompous attitude of the black man. It makes no difference to him because he is not settling in the country.

Schweitzer seems rather tired these days. His diet is mainly vegetable and I notice he refuses meat usually, but does eat fish not infrequently. He always seems to eat a number of small vegetable helpings, carrot, egg, breadfruit, eggplant, turnips etc. This must be a very good diet for an old man. He also spends a lot of time these days in the pharmacy, and he is usually writing something or other. He is very much concerned now with the atomic bomb.

Saturday June 1st: Dr Bernard left for Belgian Congo with his loaded truck. Loaded on a piroque. Schweitzer did not approve of this at all. Resented vehicle being brought near the hospital. Preferred rather for truck to remain on the island. Schweitzer resents mechanization apparently. He probably feels that it interferes with the normal routine of his hospital. Note, he also does not favour motor boats.

Speaking to Schweitzer this evening, I asked him if cannibalism still existed hereabouts. He made an odd reply. He said that he did not think he should tell me this. I don't know if his reply was to be taken literally or figuratively. Speaking to Dr Freidman *[sic]*, he also could not interpret the reply, but favoured the literal one, in that ten years ago there was a case of cannibalism in the hospital but with certain qualifications. A few insane patients dug up a recently buried native baby.

Schweitzer was also shown the new instruments and how they worked. I inspected their reserve stocks of instruments. I was amazed at the number of antiquated instruments stored away, all beautifully displayed and vaselined. I am sure these old instruments, mostly French, could form the nucleus of a wonderful surgical instrument museum.

Sunday June 2nd: News came through that Mme Schweitzer had died in Europe.[142] On asking how he took it, I was told by Ali, "in his usual manner". Presumably he takes news of all sorts very phlegmatically. No announcement at all was made.

That night being my last evening in Lambarene, I was asked to call at his room at 6pm. He gave me signed pictures, and maps of the hospital. I was also given a small elephant carving. I understand that Schweitzer gives this only on some occasions, jokingly knows as the "order of the elephant". This meeting was not the occasion for any discussion because of the news of the day. I of course did not also ask him to play the piano. He does this for the last evening with the visitor if requested.

During the afternoon, I went with Margaret in a piroque to see the papyrus swamps. Words cannot describe the beauty and enchantment of these swamps. It is truly primeval. The water is still, shiny

---

[142] She died in Zurich on 1 June 1957.

black, and the silence of the place is absolute, except for the twittering of the birds, or when something drops into the water from above e.g. from a tree, with a plop. The reflection of the trees and the papyrus swamps is too magnificent. I was only sorry I had not seen these swamps before because I would definitely have returned again to see them. The beauty I believe would be ideal for ciné filming. The water is like a weaving pattern among the islands of papyrus plants, but the piroque rower seems to know his way about. Hundreds of years ago, the landscape must have been identically the same. Nothing has changed it.

Mention should be made of two other points about the hospital. One is the goats. At night they are locked up in their pens. In the morning the gates are opened, and all the goats go streaming about, each to their individual and favourite spots. In the early morning, I used to be awakened by the clippity-clop of their hooves as they walked on the veranda past my door. The love of animals is marked by all. Ali Silver sleeps with three antelopes plus a dog in her room at night.

At meals, the tables are usually depleted considerably mainly because everybody takes food for their pets.

The second feature regarding the hospital concerns one with organization. On the last day of each month, an *appèl* is held. The purpose is to review all the cases in the hospital. Questions such as whether further treatment is required, or whether lodgers have slipped into the premises, or whether someone has not left as requested, or left without permission, are clarified.

Monday 3rd June: Left Lambarene at 8 am. Was seen off by Dr Schw, Mathilda,[143] Ali, Friedman, Catchford,[144] Vollenhoven, Olga,[145] Madelaine,[146]

---

[143] Aside from Schweitzer and perhaps Ali Silver, Mathilde Kottmann (1897-1973) was the most important person there whom my father met (aside from "Mme Schweitzer"). She was the first nurse to arrive in Lambaréné on 18 July 1924 and had been central to Schweitzer's work ever since.

[144] He means Dr Catchpool.

[145] He doesn't mention Olga Deterding's identity (see Chapter 6 above) but it's hard to believe that he remained uninformed.

[146] The Swiss Madeleine Beerli worked at the hospital from 13 October 1955 to 4 July 1957. Urquhart described her as having "a delicate fawn-like quality." In a letter to Dr van der Kreek from Günsbach (23 August 1955), Schweitzer writes that she will depart for Lambaréné soon after van Beeck-Vollenhoven departs. Miss Beerli "is not a registered nurse, but she understands medicine and worked with the Red Cross during

Varina [sic].[147] Wonderful sight to see the big three,

Schw, Mathilda and Ali standing together as you go

off. Seen off at Fr. way station by Margaret.

Air France plane left at 10 a.m. Long journey

taking about 7 ½ hrs [to Brazzaville]. Lunched at

Mouila where we wasted 1 ½ hrs. Lunch was very

good considering that Mouila is really plumb in the

bundu.[148] Lunch consisted of hors d'oeuvres (sardine

and beetroot, red cabbage, and green chile), ravioli,

sirloin, cheese, banana fritters, coffee. Meal very

cleanly served in a large sort of hut. Drinks available

as well. Much use is made of light wood structures: no

windows with glass required. Places called at *en route*

---

the War. She assisted Frau Martin for a few weeks in Günsbach, and quickly acclimatized."

[147] Urquhart (1957) described the Swiss "house officer", Verena Schmidt, as one of the "pillars of the establishment". She ran the vegetable garden, kitchens and laundry with two others. They were all young and attractive, "with no resemblance to the strait-laced types so often associated with a life of service." She was at the hospital from 17 May 1952 to 30 March 1955, from 30 August 1955 to 29 August 1958, and from 12 February 1960 to 15 November 1961.

[148] *Bundu:* A colloquial term for "bush", derived from the southern African Shona word for "grasslands".

were, after Mouila, [T]Chibanga, Mzoula, Pointe

Noire, Dolisie, and finally Brazzaville.[149]

At Brazzaville, a pleasant surprise was in store for

me. I was met by Mr Lundgren of the Swedish

Mission,[150] who offered to put me up for the night.

This was gladly accepted. I had a large suite at my

disposal. Mrs Lundgren keeps the mission spotless.

Delightful dinner and breakfast in the Swedish style.

Met other missionaries, young fellows. Was very

grateful. Mr Lundgren had arranged the air passage,

and generally made the necessary arrangements.

---

[149] Pointe Noire, Dolisie and Brazzaville are at some distance from each other in the Republic of the Congo.

[150] Head of the Mission Covenant Church of Sweden, established in Brazzaville, French Congo, in 1911, Manne Lundgren (1898-1975) occupied a diplomatic space between religion and politics. On 15 July 1961 Jaspard Kimbolo and Daniel Ndoundou (1911-1986), the latter a close colleague of Lundgren's, co-founded the revivalist Evangelical Church of Congo, an extension of the Swedish Mission. At the time, former priest, President Fulbert Youlou, was an ally of Tshombe who was fighting for neighboring Katanga's independence against UN troops, including Swedes. Youlou felt compelled to expel all Swedes. Representatives in Stockholm immediately flew out to meet with Youlou, Kimbolo, Ndoundou and Lundgren. Youlou relented. Lundgren subsequently had occasion to call on Ndoundou's help to restore peace when a crowd threatened his life. Later, when Ndoundou toured Sweden preaching with much success, Lundgren was his host and interpreter.

Epilogue

Letter from Dr Albert Schweitzer, 30 July 1961

[Handwritten. Here translated from the German.]

Mr Cecil Morris, M.Ch.   Johannesburg
302 Lister Buildings, Jeppe Street

Dear Mr Morris

We are not forgetting your visit in Lambarene, and hope that you will repeat this visit, which would bring us great joy.

Thank you for all the effort that you made regarding the prosthetic. It fits very well and the patient is very happy.

The firm has been very friendly and has given the prosthetic as a gift. That is touching. We have written to them to thank them. Miss Elsa Boer is writing to the firm because of the prosthetics of a different amputee. This one should not be given as a gift. The firm should send us the invoice and then we will send the amount.

> In the hope of seeing you again in Lambarene,
> With the best thoughts,
> Yours faithfully,
> Albert Schweitzer.

Letter from Elsje Boers, 30 July 1961

[Sent in the same envelope as Schweitzer's letter.]

Lambarene
30th July 1961.

Dear Mr Morris

What a lovely surprise! About 10 days ago Mlle.
Mathilde called me to her room and showed me a
huge box. I had no idea what it was about. Then I
opened it and saw the artificial leg – and a beautiful
one too. I was quite speechless – as I had heard no
more about it. I wondered whether my letter had not
arrived, or whether there had been a hitch
somewhere else. Bernard was duly called and was
also awed by the sudden arrival. I had told him it
might take a long time. They certainly made and sent
it promptly.

It was a wonderful experience fixing the leg,
watching him trying it out – still feeling very insecure
and the faces and expressions of the African
"infermiers" who came to see this miracle. He did not
give himself much time to get used to it and wanted to
walk about straight away. Once out of the "pharmacie"
he was soon surrounded by a shrieking crowd who
wanted to see how it was fixed on to him and how it
worked. Most proudly he showed them how he could
bend and straighten the knee. The native word for
Thank you ABORRA was constantly being repeated –
such was their gratitude for what had been done for

Bernard. The very next day he managed to walk to Dr Schweitzer's room and proudly showed off his leg to Dr Schweitzer and Mlle Mathilde. He is now able to get about quite well – and no longer sleeps with his leg on – which he did the first night!

I have also written to E.J. Reid to thank them and will ask Dr Schweitzer to add a few words himself. Did they donate the leg? Now of course Dr Friedman has found a patient who has a below knee amputation and asks if we can also have a limb made for him. Why he did not mention this patient when I asked him if he had anyone who could do with a limb I don't know. Anyway I promised to ask you – I shall leave a measurement chart with him and you can perhaps let him or me know what the situation is. Perhaps the hospital could pay – perhaps E.J. Reid wants to donate another leg! I am leaving in about 2 weeks so will not be able to get a reply from you before I leave, but as I suggest, you could let Freidman *[sic]* know.

I have had a wonderful time here – and am in a way sorry to be leaving but am still convinced that more experience would be a great asset. My European plans are not yet very definite, shall wait until I am in Europe before making really definite plans.

Thank you again for getting the making of the leg organised – it was wonderful to have been able to play a part in this giving of such a wonderful gift.

Hoping you are well – not too much work to do.

Best wishes. My neck is behaving well.

> Thank you again,
>> Sincerely
>>> Elsje Boers.

Letter from Ali Silver, 26 February 1964

[Rubber stamp with purple ink]
Dr. Albert SCHWEITZER
Lambaréné
République Gabonaise
[Underneath, written by hand]
26.2.1964

Dr. and Mrs. Cecil Morris,
1107 Lancet Hall,
Jeppe Street, Johannesburg.

Dear Dr. and Mrs. Morris,

Here come just a few lines, because you should know, that you are not forgotten in Lambarene and that we were most pleased to hear from you and receive your best wishes for the New Year. Of course we hope so much, that Dr. Schweitzer will be in our midst once more during this year. He is active, in good health and interested in every detail of the hospital work. Nobody believes that Dr. Schweitzer is in his 90th year.

We are all well. The number of patients and the number of buildings is ever growing, everywhere is activity. It would be nice to see you here again, but South Africans cannot travel to Gabon, unfortunately.

Do believe however in our kindest thoughts.

Sincerely yours,

(Miss) Ali Silver.

References

Anderson, Erica, *The Schweitzer Album: a portrait in words and pictures* (Harper, 1965).

Arlen, A. and M. Arlen, *The Huntress: The Adventures, Escapades, and Triumphs of Alicia Patterson* (Pantheon, 2016).

Berman, Edgar, *In Africa with Schweitzer* (Harper and Row, 1986).

Brabazon, James, *Albert Schweitzer: a comprehensive biography* (1976; Syracuse, 2000).

Brodmann, Roman, *"Die Wahrheit über Lambaréné"* in *Zürcher Woche*, 2 (10 January, 1964).

Cameron, James, *Point of Departure* (1967; Oriel, 1985).

O'Neil, Pat Cavendish, *A Lion in the Bedroom* (Park Street Press, 2004)

Cicovacki, Predrag (ed.), *Albert Schweitzer's Ethical Vision: A Sourcebook* (O.U.P., 2009).

Cohen, George, "The radiological demonstration of Dracunculus medinensis", *South African Medical Journal* (26 December 1959), pp. 1094-5.

Cousins, Norman, *Dr Schweitzer of Lambaréné* (Harper, 1960).

Darroch, Sandra Jobson, *Ottoline: Life of Lady Ottoline Morrell* (Cassell, 1988).

David, Anthony, *An Improbable Friendship: the story of Yasser Arafat's mother-in-law,* [and] *the wife of Israel's top general, and their 40-year mission of peace* (Simon & Schuster, 2015).

de Witte, Ludo, *The Assassination of Lumumba* (1999; Verso, 2001).

Emane, Augustin, *Albert Schweitzer: une icône africaine* (Paris: Fayard, 2013).

Fazzi, Dario, *Eleanor Roosevelt and the Anti-Nuclear Movement* (Macmillan, 2016).

Franck, Frederick, *Days with Albert Schweitzer: a Lambaréné landscape* (1959; Greenwood, 1974).

Friedman, Lawrence J., *The Lives of Erich Fromm: Love's Prophet* (Columbia U.P., 2013).

Goldwyn, R. M. and M.B. Constantian, "The Goldwyn Diary of November and December 1960, at the Albert Schweitzer Hospital, Lambaréné", *Plastic and Reconstructive Surgery*, 129:1 (January 2012), pp. 281-3.

Greene, Benjamin P., *Eisenhower, Science Advice, and the Nuclear Test-ban Debate, 1945-1963 (*Stanford Nuclear Age Series, 2006).

Jeal, Tim, *Stanley: The Impossible Life of Africa's Greatest Explorer* (Yale, 2008).

Jilek-Aall, Louise, *Working with Dr Schweitzer* (Hancock House, 1990).

Kennedy, Michael and Art Magennis, *Ireland, the United Nations and the Congo: a military and diplomatic history, 1960–1961* (Four Courts, 2014).

Kingsolver, Barbara, *The Poisonwood Bible* (Harper, 1998).

Kraft, Joy W., *The Cincinnati Zoo and Botanical Garden* (Arcadia, 2010).

Marson, Leatrice L., *Hearts from Heaven: Love from the Afterlife* (Inspiring Voices, 2014).

Marxsen, Patti, *Hélène Schweitzer: A Life of Her Own* (Syracuse University Press, 2015).

Miller, Rhena, "Albert Schweitzer and his nuclear concerns seen today" in *Courier,* XXI, 2 (Fall 1986), pp.17-26.

_____ , (ed.), *The Albert Schweitzer – Hélène Bresslau Letters 1902-1912* (Syracuse University Press, 2003).

Mühlstein, Verena, *Hélène Schweitzer Bresslau: Ein Leben für Lambaréné* (Beck, 2001).

Nies-Berger, Edouard, "Albert Schweitzer as I knew him" in *The Complete Organ series, no. 5* (Pendragon Press, 2002).

Preminger, Marion, *All I Want is Everything* (Funk & Wagnalls, 1957).

Russell, Mrs Charles E.B. [Lilian Rigby], *The Path to Reconstruction* (1941; A&C Black,1943).

Sartre, Jean-Paul, *Les Mots* (George Braziller, 1963).

Schweitzer, Albert, *J. S. Bach, Le Musicien-Poète*, introd. C. M. Widor, (Breitkopf & Härtel, 1905).

_____ , *The Quest of the Historical Jesus: a critical study of its progress from Reimarus to Wrede* (Augsburg Fortress, 1906).

_____ , *Paul and his Interpreters: a critical history,* tr. W. Montgomery (Adam & Charles Black, 1912).

_____ , *The Psychiatric Study of Jesus* (1913), his doctoral thesis.

_____ , *On the Edge of the Primeval Forest* (1922; Black, 1924).

_____ , *The Decay and Restoration of Civilization* and *Civilization and Ethics* (Black, 1923); published together as *Philosophy and Civilization* (Macmillan, 1949).

_____ , *Indian Thought and its Development* (H. Holt, 1936).

_____ , *Afrikanische Geschichten* (Felix Meiner, 1938); tr. Mrs C. E. B. Russell, *From My African Notebook* (Allen and Unwin, 1938).

_____ , *Peace or Atomic War?* (H. Holt, 1958).

_____ , *Ein Pelikan erzählt aus seinem Leben* [A pelican recounts his life] (Hamburg, 1950); tr. Martha Wardenburg, *The Story of My Pelican* (Souvenir, 1964).

Soret, Marcel, *Démographie et problèmes urbains en A.E.F.* (*Mémoires de l'institut d'études centralafricaines,* 1954).

Urquhart, Clara, *With Dr Schweitzer in Lambaréné* (Harrap, 1957).

Williams, Susan, *Spies in the Congo: the race for the ore that built the atomic bomb* (Hurst, 2016).

Wittner, Lawrence S., "Blacklisting Schweitzer", *Bulletin of Atomic Scientists* (May-June 1995), pp. 55-60.

Zoellner, Tom, *Uranium: War, Energy, and the Rock that Shaped the World* (Penguin, 2009).

....

Index

178

T. A. C.
LONDON